The Policy Participation of Business Associations in China

Yongdong Shen

The Policy Participation of Business Associations in China

ZHEJIANG UNIVERSITY PRESS
浙江大学出版社

palgrave
macmillan

Yongdong Shen
School of Public Affairs, Academy
of Social Governance
Zhejiang University
Hangzhou, China

ISBN 978-981-96-1095-2 ISBN 978-981-96-1096-9 (eBook)
https://doi.org/10.1007/978-981-96-1096-9

Jointly published with Zhejiang University Press
The print edition is not for sale in Mainland of China. Customers from Mainland of China please order the print book from: Zhejiang University Press.
ISBN of the Co-Publisher's edition: 978-7-308-23178-7

This book was supported by the Zhejiang Province "Pioneer" and "Leading Goose" R&D Program (grant number: 2024C03268), Major Program of Philosophy and Social Science of Chinese Ministry of Education (grant number: 21JZD019, 2023JZDZ038), National Natural Science Foundation of China (grant number: 72022016, 71704156).

This Palgrave Macmillan imprint is published by the registered company Springer Nature Singapore Pte Ltd.
The registered company address is: 152 Beach Road, #21-01/04 Gateway East, Singapore 189721, Singapore

Foreword

This book, *The Policy Participation of Business Associations in China*, is the research achievement of Dr. Shen Yongdong. Dr. Shen has devoted himself to studying industry associations and chambers of commerce since joining my team in 2009, and this original research achievement reveals his strong interest in China's political and business relations.

The policy participation of Chinese industry associations and chambers of commerce is an essential window into the relationship between politics and business in contemporary China. In 2014, Dr. Shen and I co-authored the first English paper on the policy participation of industry associations and chambers of commerce: "Autonomy or Privilege? Lobbying Intensity of Local Business Associations in China". It was published in the *Journal of Chinese Political Science* and praised and cited by well-known scholars like Gunter Schubert, Thomas Heberer, Marian R. Chertow, Junming Zhu, etc.

Since then, this intensive fieldwork has culminated in the book-length research dissertation "Strategic Interactions between Industry Associations and Governments in a Changing Environment". And, with the changes made during the 19th National Congress of the Communist Party of China in 2017, the policy participation of industry associations and chambers of commerce has become part of the democratic consultation process among social organizations. They now play a more critical role in China's economic and social governance. Based on this new understanding, Dr. Shen revised his doctoral dissertation to this work.

Dr. Shen's work strives to answer some core questions about policy participation by industry associations and chambers of commerce. At the beginning of the book, the author asks: "How exactly does an industry association or chamber of commerce participate in policy work in China?" "What factors influence contemporary Chinese industry associations and chambers of commerce?" "How do Chinese industry associations and chambers of commerce interact with government?" Guided by these questions, Dr. Shen discusses the characteristics of policy participation of these important industry representatives, the factors influencing them, and the types of political-government interactions they employ.

The policy participation of China's industry associations and chambers of commerce is characterized by the diversity of target audiences, the diversification of policy participation channels and strategies, and the effectiveness of policy participation results. Government policy willingness, industry associations and chambers of commerce policy participation ability, and good external environment are the key factors affecting the policy participation behavior of industry associations and chambers of commerce in China.

After a statistical analysis of a large sample of data and a comparative case analysis, Dr. Shen arrived at an essential point of view that the policy participation of industry associations and chambers of commerce is the result of a two-way strategic interaction between the government and these two groups in a changing environment.

The development of China's industry associations and chambers of commerce has entered a new era of continuous improvement driven by the external environment. In June 2018, the General Office of the Central Committee of the Communist Party of China and the General Office of the State Council issued the "Implementation Opinions on Promoting the Reform and Development of Chambers of Commerce Affiliated to the Federation of Industry and Commerce" to examine various measures for the reform and development of chambers of commerce affiliated with the All-China Federation of Industry and Commerce. The policy's purpose is to explore and innovate the governance and operation mode of the nation's chambers of commerce. Important instructions have been promulgated to improve their functional roles and strengthen their institutionalization and standardization.

In January 2019, the Supreme People's Court and the All-China Federation of Industry and Commerce jointly issued the "Opinions on Leveraging the Mediation Advantages of Chambers of Commerce to

Promote the Construction of a Diversified Resolution Mechanism for Disputes in the Private Economy". The document is meant to give play to the advantages of chambers of commerce in mediation and promote the construction of a diversified resolution mechanism for disputes in the private economy, indicating that Chambers of commerce have also expanded their role from industry management to social governance. In March 2019, the General Office of the State Council issued the "Notice on Fully Hearing the Opinions of Enterprises and Industry Associations and Chambers of Commerce in the Process of Formulating Administrative Regulations and Administrative Normative Documents". Within this policy directive is the power to make institutional arrangements for industry associations and chambers of commerce to participate in the formulation of regulations and policies. In effect, it is an external institutional guarantee that the industry associations and chambers of commerce can advocate for social and economic policies, participate in their formulation and implementation, and mediate disputes.

The Fourth Plenary Session of the 19th Central Committee of the Communist Party of China decided several significant issues meant to improve and modernize the nation's socialist system with Chinese characteristics. Its stated goals include greater self-discipline in industry associations and chambers of commerce, constructive interactions between government governance, social adjustment, and residents' self-governance, and the consolidation of the foundation of social governance.

As the external institutional environments of China's industry associations and chambers of commerce improve, their capacity building has been increasingly put on the policy agenda of higher-level governments and the chambers of commerce themselves. To show their support for industry associations and chambers of commerce, some local governments have taken the following actions, including, holding training courses, formulating catalogs for government purchasing, and launching support policies and special funds for them. In some pioneering areas, industry associations and chambers of commerce have also actively created industry trademarks to build social influence, set up a "government-to-business express train" to directly deliver the voices and needs of private enterprises to local government leaders, and jointly made a local office to explore multiple mediation mechanisms for collaborative governance.

In general, the capacities of industry associations and chambers of commerce must be built both internally and externally. From an internal perspective, industry associations and chambers of commerce need to improve their organizational capabilities such as governance structure, strategic and project management, and evaluation and incentive systems. From an external perspective, industry associations and chambers of commerce need to strengthen their external capabilities such as cooperation, coordination, and alliances with the government, enterprises, and other social organizations. The governance capacities of the industry associations and chambers of commerce can only be improved through the joint efforts of not only the government and the chambers of commerce, but also experts and scholars.

In 2001, Professor Jinglian Wu, a well-known economist in China, initiated the "China Non-Government Chamber of Commerce Forum". Its goals are to enhance the capacity of industry associations and chambers of commerce and to build a platform for interactions with external stakeholders. Every year, the forum selects a theme and invites domestic and foreign experts and scholars, practitioners from chambers of commerce and industry associations, and leaders of relevant party and government departments to conduct in-depth discussions. Since 2013, the forum has been permanently settled in Zhejiang province and hosted by the School of Public Administration of Zhejiang University in conjunction with relevant units and institutions. Zhejiang Province and its capital, Hangzhou, are the best and were the earliest developers of a private economy and non-government chamber of commerce in post-Mao China. This provides a strong practical foundation for Zhejiang University's Chamber of Commerce research team to lead the country.

The book is one of a series of achievements of our Zhejiang University Business Association Research Team. I warmly recommend this book to international readers and call on colleagues who are interested in the research and practice of industry associations and chambers of commerce to engage with the policy participation, reform, and development of these groups in China.

Hangzhou, Zhejiang Province, China
November 2019

Yu Jianxing

Contents

About the Author

Yongdong Shen is a Professor at School of Public Affairs, Zhejiang University. He is the Deputy Dean of Academy of Social Governance at Zhejiang University and a distinguished research fellow of Institute of State System Research at Zhejiang University. His research focuses on nonprofit organizations and government relations in non-Western settings. He has published articles in journals like *Public Administration Review, Public Management Review, Nonprofit and Voluntary Sector Quarterly, and China Quarterly.*

List of Tables

Chapter 6

CHAPTER 1

Introduction

An effective way to know and understand a state–society relationship is to study those industry associations and chambers of commerce that participate in policy formulation and revision. From the decision-making models of "one-man show" and "bureaucratic pluralism", to "fragmented authoritarianism" and "consultative government", and then to "consensus-based decision-making", the formulation and introduction of policy in contemporary China is no longer just a top-down manifestation of the government's will. Rather, the process has become the arena in which national and social interests are expressed and their advocates compete for attention and resources (Oksenberg, 2001; Chen, 2012; Wang and Fan, 2013). As a result, the state–society relationship has evolved out of the previous state–society dichotomy and has been transformed into state–society interaction.

In October 2017, General Secretary Xi Jinping in his report to the 19th National Congress of the Communist Party of China noted the importance of social organizations in deliberative democracy and coordinated consultations with these groups should be promoted. This shows that these groups have already participated in notable ways in policy negotiations. Industry associations and chambers of commerce are the largest social organizations in China. Because they are non-governmental, economical, low-risk, and have high legitimacy. They actively participate in policy creation that can take the form of laws, regulations, policy recommendations, or industry standards. In 2013 alone, national industry

Y. Shen, *The Policy Participation of Business Associations in China*,
https://doi.org/10.1007/978-981-96-1096-9_1

associations and chambers of commerce put forward a total of 1729 policy recommendations to government departments on behalf of various industries and member companies, of which 912 were adopted. They participated in the revision and formulation of 392 laws and regulations in the formulation of 5549 standards, of which 202 items were used to participate in the formulation of international standards and rules. Given their prominence in this area, an examination of the relationship between the state and society through the policy participation of contemporary Chinese industry associations and chambers of commerce is of relevance. It allows us to explore the evolution, diversification, and dynamics of the interaction between the state and society.

The questions this book attempts to answer include: How exactly do contemporary Chinese industry associations and chambers of commerce participate in policy formation? What factors have influenced that participation? In the process of policy participation and practice, how do they interact with the government? What types of state–society relations do these interactions between the two create? How can this exploration contribute to our understanding of the diversity and dynamics of state–society interactions in China?

This study is informed by empirical research of a large sample of descriptive data on the policy participation of Chinese industry associations and chambers of commerce. The statistical analysis shows these groups target diverse policy objects and participate using different approaches and strategies. Nearly one-third of the industry associations and chambers of commerce studied here either successfully influenced policy formulation and revision in their interactions with the government, or made the government stop the implementation of a policy. The results of a large-sample regression analysis reveal that the policy participation capacity of industry associations and chambers of commerce had an impact on the frequency of policy participation, but it was not significant. Instead, the government's policy had a significant impact on the policy participation of these two groups. The results of a comparative study of multiple cases show that their policy participation took diverse paths. Their ability to participate in policy formation is the foundation, while the willingness of local governments to allow them to voice their opinions is the core of successful policy participation. Successful policy participation requires a proper external environment that encourages engagement with the government. In contemporary China, this participatory ecosystem is a dual initiative and two-way interaction between industry associations and chambers of commerce and the government.

Based on a large sample of data and a comparative case analysis, this book interprets the diversification and dynamics of contemporary Chinese state–society interactions as two-way strategic interactions between the state and society in a changing external environment. In different external environments, the state and society each promote their own initiatives, using existing rules and resources as construction actions.

Due to the complexity and variability of the external environment, social subjects need to adopt different strategies to deal with changes in the external environment. The state will also adjust in accordance with those strategies and changes in the external environment.

The remainder of this book is structured as follows. The second chapter sorts out the theory of contemporary Chinese state–society relations, presents the relevant research, shows how it has changed, and examines its insufficiencies and defects regarding the relationship between China's industry associations and chambers of commerce and the government. It also suggests new ways to analyze the mechanisms by which these groups interact with each other. The third chapter constructs an analytical framework of the "two-way strategic interaction between government and industry associations and chambers of commerce in a changing external environment" and puts forward the study's research hypotheses. Chapter 4 explains the research samples, data sources, questionnaire design and distribution, as well as the basic content and object selection of the case studies. Chapter 5 describes the policy participation of contemporary Chinese industry associations and chambers of commerce based on an analysis of a large data sample. After examining the institutional objects, diversification strategies, attitudes, and actual impact effects, the chapter then explores the statistical relationship among the ability of the sampled industry associations and chambers of commerce to participate in policy practice, the government's expressions of its policy will, and the frequency of policy participation by industry associations and chambers of commerce.

In Chapter 6, through in-depth case interviews and multi-case comparative study, the diversified and dynamic interactions between industry associations, chambers of commerce, and the government through policy participation and the mechanism behind it are shown. The closing chapter concludes with a discussion that briefly summarizes the book's findings and contributions, examines its shortcomings, and presents directions for future research.

References

Chen S. Changes in China's Public Policy Model Based on the Analytical Perspective of Interest Groups. Journal of Social Sciences, 2012, 8: 13-23.

Oksenberg M. China's political system: Challenges of the twenty-first century. The China Journal, 2001, 45: 21-35.

Wang S, and Fan P. Chinese consensus-based decision-making: opening doors and harmonization. Beijing: People's University of China Press, 2013.

CHAPTER 2

Chinese Industry Associations and Chambers of Commerce: Research from the Perspective of State–Society Relations

Scholars have noted a transition in state–society relations theory from the state–society dichotomy to the state–society interaction. This change makes it necessary to explore why the relationship between the state and society in contemporary China is pluralistic and dynamic.

This chapter, from the perspective of state–society relations theory, discusses the existing theoretical literature with industry associations and chambers of commerce as the research object. After reviewing the two theories of structural debate and dynamic analysis, it then shows how the relationships between the government and industry associations and chambers of commerce are diverse and dynamic. This is followed by an explanation of the deficiencies of state–society relations theory and the proposals to re-interpret it from the perspective of structure–function unity.

After examining the existing research on the policy participation of industry associations and chambers of commerce, this chapter then focuses on the research around their policy participation from the perspective of the theory of state–society relations, capturing their different modes and interaction mechanisms. The chapter concludes by proposing that the diversification and dynamics of state–society interactions in contemporary China may be the result of strategic state–society interactions in a changing environment.

Y. Shen, *The Policy Participation of Business Associations in China*,
https://doi.org/10.1007/978-981-96-1096-9_2

1 Theoretical Research on the Relationship Between State and Society in Contemporary China and Its Transformation

The relationship between the state and society is a long-term concern of scholars of contemporary China. The state–society dichotomy and the relationship between state and society as zero-sum game were once the main research paradigms of state and society (Gilley 2011; Kuhn 1996). Among them, state-centrism and society-centrism were the two major theories of the dichotomy between the state and society. In the 1990s, things shifted. State–society relations researchers began to examine state–society relations in more nuanced ways. Many chose to observe such interactions from the state, the social, or the cooperative perspectives, among others

1.1 Research on the Dichotomous Relationship Between the State and Society

After the founding of the People's Republic in 1949, Chinese society spent 30 years under a strong state. The economic planning system and the social "unit system" led to ubiquitous state control over society. With the reform and opening up, the development of the market economy and the expansion of social space, social forces were able to emerge and develop. Despite this, China has not fundamentally changed its state-based model. The separation of the state and society and the zero-sum relationship between them remain verdant scholarly fields.

1.1.1 State-Centric Theory

The state-centered research paradigm has become the dominant paradigm (see footnote 1) for overseas scholars to interpret Chinese politics. This research paradigm considers the state or the Chinese Communist Party ("Party") to be the dominant factor in any series of events. Most of these studies focus on the macro-political system and political legitimacy. Representative works include: "Fragmented Authoritarianism" (Lieberthal and Lampton 1992); "Consultative Leninism" (Tsang 2009); "Adaptive Authoritarianism", and "Authoritarian: From the perspective of state-society relations, Resilient Authoritarianism" (Nathan 2003).

Kenneth Lieberthal constructed a model of "fragmented authoritarianism" after researching bureaucracy and policy-making in China. He believed that under China's political system, government departments control specific resources, thus making it difficult for the central leadership to effectively direct policy outcomes (Lieberthal 1992). In that same vein, David M. Lampton argued that China's fragmented bureaucracy "dilutes" the process of political implementation so much so that the central government must bargain with various ministries and local government departments to better obtain cooperation and implement policies (Lampton 1987).

Fragmented authoritarianism is regarded as a state-centered research theory because it only considers the bureaucracy's fragmentation of the bureaucracy from the state's perspective when examining China's policy formulation and implementation. Andrew Mertha's supplementary study argues that the institutional process of China's policymaking is multivariate; he called it "fragmented authoritarianism 2.0" (Mertha 2009). Steve Tsang proposed the concept of "consultative Leninism", in which the Party experiences social and political challenges but Leninism makes the political machine more resilient by incorporating consultative elements (Tsang 2009). However, "consultative Leninism" emphasizes "consultation" as a key factor in times when the Party and the state are under heavy external pressure, such as a financial crisis, to maintain political power and enhance its governance capacity. But, because the impacts of these "consultative elements" on the Party or the country are never accounted for, it is still a state-centered research paradigm.

Research on the state's adjustments to society's awakening began with Andrew J. Nathan, who believed system is resilient rather than fragile given the regular rotation and retirement of top leaders, the merit system for cadre promotion, the functional differentiation and specialization of institutions, and the development of political participation that enhances the adaptability and viability of state power (Nathan 2003). Later, Bruce J. Dickson, Kellee S. Tsai, and others investigated the relationship between Chinese private entrepreneurs and the Party. They believed that the Party effectively eliminated private entrepreneurs' concerns by co-opting them as Party members and making them deputies to the People's Congress or members of the Political Consultative Conference. This was to eliminate too much scrutiny of the unfavorable factors in the regime (Dickson 2003; Tsai 2007). Yang Dali suggested that by paying attention, and responding, to social needs, China can adaptively respond to the pressures of economic and social development (Yang 2004).

Most of these studies analyze the Chinese political system with the state or Party as the main body of analysis, and they are considered very persuasive in the study of state/society relations.

1.1.2 Socio-Centrism

With the transformation and development of China's economy and society, research approaches such as socio-centrism and the interaction between the state and society have begun to emerge, challenging the long-dominant state-centered theory. This change in thinking has focused research on China's market economy, social organizations, and individual citizens. Society has become the core driving force for reforms and event-inspired changes.

Lynn T. White suggests that China's reforms are initiated by social forces. After the Cultural Revolution, the lack of national capacity and the weakening of state-owned enterprises provided opportunities for township enterprises to absorb surplus labor and pursue their own interests (White 1998). Kate X. Zhou views China's farmers as the driving force for China's economic development and social change. They created a household contract responsibility system based on their own interests, created new markets, established township enterprises, and broke through the government's monopoly on organizing, and this household registration control played a leading role in China's economic reform and development (Zhou 1996).

Some studies have also begun to focus on the local level. For example, as shown in her study of Wenzhou, Kristen Parris believes the city's residents took steps to develop the private economy as early as the 1960s and 1970s. This was due to local changes. The promotion of self-employed workers, family workshops, and social groups in pursuit of their own interests was one result of the planned economy's failure to meet local needs (Parris 1993). Socially effective institutional innovation often precedes formal national reforms. Reforms, changes, and innovative practices developed by society have been recognized by the central government and become national policies. They are called Adaptive Informal Institutions (Tsai 2006).

Another scholarly view seeks out a Western-style civil society in China that is antagonistic to the state. It emphasizes the independence of society from the state and tries to find a "Chinese citizen society" that can confront or balance the state to promote democratization. Ostergaard first used the "theory of civil society against the state" to explain the nation's political turmoil in the late 1980s, which then triggered the discussion of the applicability of civil society to China (Gu Xin 1994). In the process of their search, Gordon White and others found "civil society" to have a diverse and fragmented impact on society. It became both a driving force and an obstacle to democratization (White, Howell and Xiaoyuan 1996). He believes China has a "semi-civil society" that can provide a haven for democratizing forces and democrats and a support force for social stability and neo-authoritarianism (He 1996, 1997). Although there is not much research literature on socio-centrism, it has had an impact that presents a sharp challenge to the dominant Chinese political science research paradigm of state-centrism.

1.2 The Interaction Between the State and Society

Since the 1990s, the international academic community has gradually broken the state–society dichotomy. Joel S. Migdal's "State in Society" (Migdal 2001), Peter B. Evans' "Embedded Autonomy" (Evans 1995), "Co-governance of State and Society" (Evans 1997), etc., hold that the state and society are not dichotomous. On the contrary, the relationship is both cooperative and complementary, and its dynamism can even shape and entangle them in unforeseen ways. The shift of the international academic community from a static structural perspective of the state–society dichotomy to a dynamic process perspective has had a profound impact on the study of China's state–society relations. Different from the single research paradigms such as "state-centered theory" and "socio-centered theory", contemporary Chinese studies have also begun to explore issues from the perspective of the interaction between the state and society.

Vivienne Shue proposes that this research perspective focuses on the "interaction between the state and society as conditions for each other" (Shue 2008). The mutual adjustment of state and society is at the "core of the post-Chinese political experience" (Baum and Shevchenko 1999). Elizabeth J. Perry also believes that, since the 1990s, China's early "authoritarianism" and other theoretical models have begun to give way to the exploration of the complex relationship between the state and society (Perry 1994). However, even from the perspective of state–society interactions, research on the state–society relationship in China still finds it difficult to resolve debates on the degree of state control over society and the embedding of society into the state for legitimacy.

Some researchers still focus on either the state or society, resulting in three perspectives under the state–society interaction theory: a state perspective, a social perspective, and a cooperative perspective.

1.2.1 The Interaction Between the State and Society: The State Perspective

This perspective emphasizes that society has grown inside the state. Although there are interactive behaviors between them, the state still plays a vital role. Typical theories include Corporatism, the Developmental or Entrepreneurial State, and Classification Control. Anita Chan and Jonathan Unger believe that China's state–society relationship is corporatist. At the national level, social organizations have developed, but the state will only recognize one specific organization (such as the All-China Federation of Trade Unions, the All-China Federation of Industry and Commerce, etc.). They alone act as the representatives of the interests of certain groups. The state decides which organization is legal and then builds a cooperative relationship through it. Some even participate in the policy-making system and might represent the government's position in the formulation of national policies (Unger and Chan 1995). Di Zhongpu agrees and suggests that China's state corporatism animates its trade associations and chambers of commerce despite their being composed of private entrepreneurs. He believes that "trade associations and chambers of commerce do not have complete autonomy but are deeply embedded in the country; their daily activities, personnel choices, and finances can be manipulated and controlled by the state" (Dickson 2008).

After studying the behavior of local governments motivated by fiscal reforms, Jean C. Oi suggests that in the process of economic development, local governments have many characteristics of companies. Officials acting as a quasi-board-of-directors within this new institutional form of government-economic integration are examples of "local corporatism" (Oi 1995).

With the liberalization of the market economy and the growth of social forces, the state began to loosen some of its control over the market and society. Jennifer Y. J. Hsu and Reza Hasmath argue that the state has by no means withdrawn from society. Its interaction with emerging social organizations suggests that the state seeks to manage changes in society. The state seeks to reaffirm its commitment to dominate society, so the essence of China's state corporatism has not changed despite economic and social growth (Hsu and Hasmath 2012).

The theory of developmental or entrepreneurial government espouses reform in the market economy so government officials will try to increase the funds available to start for-profit businesses in emerging markets. This is distinct from state-owned enterprises. Jane Duckett calls this "State Entrepreneurialism" (Duckett 2002), which aims at state adaptation. Entrepreneurial behaviors are adapted to market reforms to better reconstruct the state and control the market.

Kang Xiaoguang and Han Heng proposed a "classified control system" by examining the state's actual control over social organizations. In this system, the government serves its own interests. According to the social organization's ability to challenge the state and provide public goods, different control strategies are adopted (Kang and Han 2005). However, whether it is corporatism, the developmental or entrepreneurial state, or classification control theory, all three are intended to show that the state is still more important in any interaction between the state and society. Social organizations can only carry out limited activities within the framework set by the state.

1.2.2 The Social Perspective Under the Interaction Between the State and Society

The social perspective under the interaction between state and society emphasizes that organizations or citizens in society can play an active role in the relationship between state and society. Peter Ho and Richard L. Edmonds believe that while limiting social freedom, semi-authoritarianism also creates a social space for civic action, and social movements take place in a mosaic way in this semi-liberal environment, which is conducive to mitigating the risk of social instability and political repression (Ho and Edmonds 2007). China is a big agricultural country, with the vast majority of the population living in rural areas which often plays an important part in this research perspective. Kevin J. O'Brien and Lianjiang Li, based on their research on the specific resistance behaviors of Chinese farmers, believe that farmers, through "Rightful Resistance", urge China to provide good governance and responsive policies, which "The peasants use the gap between state promises, such as laws and regulations, state policies, villager elections, and the actual behavior of the state as a tool to safeguard their own interests (O'Brien and Li 2006)". Lily L. Tsai through her research on the supply of public services such as road maintenance and school building in different villages, found that the accountability of government officials in the provision of rural public services by the formal system is relatively weak. On the contrary, Solidary Groups, such as Lineage, etc., form moral constraints on officials' status by means of Encompassing and Embedding, thus producing effective Informal Accountability (Tsai 2007). In addition to rural areas as an important research field for scholars from this research perspective, grassroots NGOs are often the research objects of these scholars because of their unofficial and independent nature. Some scholars have explored grassroots NGOs' efforts to improve the institutional environment through informal political strategies, to achieve self-legalization, and to interact and cooperate with the government to obtain resources and achieve self-organization goals (Zhang and Zhuang 2008; Zhao 2004). Some scholars believe that environmental NGOs, media, and citizens can change the original national policies and supervise and criticize the government through civic action (Mertha 2008; Zhao 2004).

1.2.3 Benign Interaction and Cooperative Governance Between the State and Society

The cooperative perspective under the interaction between the state and society emphasizes that there is no clear boundary between the state and society. Citizen participation can strengthen the state, and state institutions create a favorable environment for citizen participation. On the one hand, certain state institutions are embedded in society. On the other hand, the public fully participates in national governance and public service provision, and realizes the co-governance of the two (Evans 1997). The win–win results of consultation and cooperation between the state and society have been confirmed by more and more scholars. Jessica C. Teets, through a case study of grassroots NGOs the Beijing Can Yushi Information Consulting Center's cooperation with local governments to provide public services to develop the ability of urban communities to participate in governance, proposes a new model of China's state–society interaction, "consultative authoritarianism", which seeks to expand the autonomous activity space of social organizations while trying to establish a new indirect social control mechanism (Teets 2013). Through empirical research on the successful construction of a farmer town in Wenzhou during the market transition period, Zhou Yi believes that China's state–society relationship is an interdependence model, which is mainly reflected in the interdependence between farmers and local governments. Moblization-Response Process and Patron-Client Ties have become collaborators, participants, and practitioners and then successfully realize the underlying institutional changes (Zhou 2013). Jing Yijia concluded that the Chinese government has adopted a dual strategy of "empowerment and control" for social organizations (Jing 2015).

In the analysis of the motivation of cooperative governance between the state and society, some scholars regard it as the result of the "alignment of interests" of social sectors, which means rent-seekers take the initiative to "entwine" (Entwinement) and the state is forced to actively open up social space to seek cooperation due to economic and social pressure. Jude Howell calls the tension between local government and labor NGOs part of a "welfare association" strategy, which aims to redefine the relationship between the state and labor social contract between them (Howell 2015). On the other hand, Shen Yongdong and Yu Jianxing attribute the cooperation between local governments and social organizations to performance-oriented cooperation (Shen and Yu 2017). Although only few cases of state–society alliances and mutually conditioned true equal cooperative relations in China today, the above-mentioned studies on benign interaction and cooperative governance have at least added a new dimension to the study of state–society relations theory.

The evolution of the above-mentioned research theories from different perspectives presents a different picture of the relationship between the state and society in China. Vivienne Shue criticized the "simplification", "too simplistic and stereotyped" and "narrow, one-dimensional and static assumptions" in contemporary Chinese political research theory (Shue 1988). Shaun Breslin believes that China is a complex object of study, and if a simple analysis model is used to understand the complex China, it is often counterproductive (Breslin 2008). The complex relationship between the state and society in China is not only because China is in a period of rapid change, but also because there are differences between the central level and the local level, the first-developing regions and the later-developing regions, and the different fields of social organization, etc. All these determine that the research on the relationship between the state and society in contemporary China needs to move from single to multiple, from static to dynamic. Therefore, it is necessary and urgent to explore the research theories of the diversification and dynamics of the relationship between the state and society in contemporary China.

2 Contemporary Chinese Chamber of Commerce Research: Structural Debate, Action Analysis, and Beyond

Since the reform and opening up, the development of China's market economy and the opening of social space have enabled social organizations (see footnote 1) to develop rapidly. Social organization is an important part of social growth and development. Many scholars at home and abroad have begun to use social organization as the research object to observe the relationship between the state and society in contemporary China and its changes, which have led to different academic debates. Some scholars have sorted out research at home and abroad into structural debate and action analysis (Wang and Song 2013; Zhang 2012). The structural debate is based on the different positions and powers of the state–society dual subject in the political space.

It is reasonable to judge that there will be a relationship of either confrontation or cooperation between state power and social forces, and then analyze the nature of China's state–society relationship from a macro level. This is mainly reflected in the debate between pluralism and corporatism: the theory of pluralism believes that it is necessary to study China's social organization from the standpoint of society, emphasizing the independence of society relative to the state, in order to construct the ability of the "public sphere" to check and balance the state Power is divided into confrontation theory and benign interaction theory (Alexander 1997; M. Edwards 2004; Deng and Alexander 1999). The theory of corporatism, from the perspective of the state, posits that in order to achieve the purpose of controlling society, the government chooses to develop special cooperative relations with specific social organizations. Organizations become bridges and media between the state and society, and an important mechanism for the party and the state to link the market and society (Schmitter 1974; Unger and Chan 1996). Action analysis focuses on the actors in the state–society relationship, arguing that the state–society relationship depends on the actor's own behavior, and then grasps the interaction mechanism and action strategy between the state and society at the micro level. Action analysis focuses on the actions of social organizations, as well as the strategies and mechanisms by which social organizations draw resources and effectively interact with the state in order to achieve self-survival, development, and social change. Structural debate and action analysis complement each other between static structure and dynamic action research, and constitute an important part of interpreting and analyzing the relationship between the state and society in China from the perspective of social organization.

Industry associations and chambers of commerce are the largest social organization among Chinese social organizations. Because of their non-governmental, independent, low-risk, high-return characteristics and nationwide organizational systems, they have become ideal research objects to observe the relationship between China's state and society (Kang and Han 2005; Wang 2006). Taking industry associations and chambers of commerce as the research object, scholars have launched important discussions on the relationship between the state and society in China from two aspects: structural debate and action analysis.

2.1 Structural Debate on the Study of Contemporary Chinese Industry Associations and Chambers of Commerce

Industry associations and chambers of commerce are the earliest developed economic and social organizations in China, and early research on them focused on the changes in China's state-social structure caused by the development of industry associations and chambers of commerce.

State–Social Relations Perspective.

It is argued that most of these studies focus on whether industry associations and chambers of commerce can generate power against the state, whether they have autonomy independent of the state, and whether they can represent the interests of their members.

2.1.1 Research on Industry Associations and Chambers of Commerce from the Perspective of Pluralism

According to the research of Michael Edwards, civil society under Western theory can be summarized into three main streams. The first underlines civil society that emphasizes associational life, which is independent of the state system and market system, and is the third sector made up of social organizations. This view is represented by Alexis de Tocqueville. The second is civil society based on value goals, which regards civil society as a good society formed by social values and moral consensus, represented by Geer. The third sees civil society as a public sphere, regards civil society as a space of public interest formed by rational communication and consensus and pursuit, and Habermas is the representative.

Edwards pointed out that "only the first school—civil society as an associational life, is the dominant thought" (Edwards 2004). Jonathan Unger also believes that "the modern revival of the concept of civil society stems from the dissident intellectuals in Eastern Europe in the 1970s and 1980s, who conceived a way to develop individual and collective freedom. In doing so, they mostly refer to the public sphere created by communal life in the conception of Antonio Gramsci and Tocqueville as civil society" (Unger 2008). As an economic society, industry associations and chambers of commerce have developed rapidly after the reform of the market economy. In the 1990s, with the emergence of new forms of organizations, industry associations and chambers of commerce broke the highly homogeneous pattern of state and society and opened a new space for social development, prompting scholars to discuss and define the so-called Chinese civil society (White et al. 1996).

Some scholars observed through the experiences of industry associations and chambers of commerce that the emergence and development of the private economy has provided necessary conditions for new associations. According to the survey, although the state still maintains a dominant and controlling position, these social and economic forces will become more independent and autonomous as the economic reform and development continues (White 1993). Some scholars have also seen that industry associations and chambers of commerce have played an important political function on behalf of the interests of their members. For example, Zhang Jianjun believes that the economic development model driven by the private economy has prompted the Wenzhou Chamber of Commerce, which is established and run by enterprises from the bottom-up, to serve the social interests of enterprises, and to serve the social interests of enterprises, to play an important function in political role (Zhang 2007). Some scholars believe that the rise and development of chambers of commerce does not mean that there is a confrontational relationship between the state and society. The chamber of commerce is neither intended to confront the government nor passive in the relationship between the state and society. On the contrary, it can positively influence the state to promote the development of social forces. Scholars such as Yu Jianxing and Zhou Jun have investigated the Wenzhou Chamber of Commerce's active participation in public affairs management and believe that the Chamber of Commerce makes full use of the government's increasingly open space to the society, obtains government empowerment, actively participates in public governance, and realizes the growth and development of social forces through participation. (Yu and Guo 2012; Yu and Zhou 2013; Yu, Zhou and Jiang 2012; Yu et al. 2008); Tony Saich also believes that, in addition to the state's Soviet-style resetting of control on society, social organizations have also adopted a strategy of negotiating with the state to readjust the relationship between the state and society, in order to reduce state penetration, allow social organization policy input, and pursue members' interests and achieve organizational goals (Saich 2000).

However, many scholars have questioned the rise and development of China's civil society from the perspective of industry associations and chambers of commerce. They believe that industry associations and chambers of commerce, being the product of the government's administrative system, lack the initiative and autonomy that society should have in both establishment and operation. For example, Christopher E. Nevitt believes that the behavior of the chamber of commerce is the result of the promotion strategy of officials, which should be viewed from the institutional perspective of the national center, with scholars focusing on the incentive behavior of officials in the party-government system to consider the role and performance of different private chambers of commerce, rather than the simple confrontation between the state and society from the perspective of civil society (Nevitt 1996). Kenneth W. Foster also proposed that when studying the Chinese Chamber of Commerce, it should be considered as a new element of the national administrative system, rather than as a participant in the dialogue between the state and society. Through his research on Yantai City, he found that almost all chambers of commerce are established by the party and government departments. In essence, the Yantai chambers of commerce are equivalent to subordinate institutions that perform tasks entrusted by the party and government departments, rather than a new field of interaction between the state and society (Foster 2002). Wank's research on Xiamen's commercial organizations found that commercial organizations are alliances between local officials and some private actions (Wank 1995). Joseph Fewsmith found through an investigation of the Wenzhou Chamber of Commerce that the Wenzhou Chamber of Commerce is only a platform for private entrepreneurs to accumulate network capital (Fewsmith 2013).

2.1.2 *Research on Industry Associations and Chambers of Commerce from the Perspective of Corporatism*

Since the 1970s, corporatism (see footnote 2), like liberalism, totalitarianism, and socialism, has been widely used in analyzing European and Asian countries as an effective theoretical tool. Philippe Schmitter was the first to define corporatism as "a mechanism of interest representation composed of a limited number of functionally differentiated interest groups", and believed that corporatism should be regarded as interests and (or) attitudes. This institutionalized structural arrangement adopts civil society into the structure of the state (Schmitter 1974). During the same period, Howard J. Wiarda pointed out that corporatism has two meanings when used: one is the institutional practice of various interests in the 1930s and 1940s; the other is a dominant form of sociopolitical organization characterized by hierarchy, elitism, and authoritarianism (Wiarda 1974). What the two scholars have in common is that they both regard corporatism as an institutional structure for the expression of interests. As a theoretical tool for analyzing the relationship between the state and society, corporatism believes that the state occupies a dominant position in the structure of interests, but its specific strength varies with different social situations. Different forms of government can be associated with corporatism: Western European countries are typical of the combination of corporatism and liberal democracies; Latin American countries use corporatism to supplement the "Bureaucratic Authoritarian Regime"; the socialist countries of Eastern Europe have also used corporatism to organize agriculture, industry, and intellectuals (Chirot 1980); corporatism also applies to explain the phenomenon that emerging East Asian countries such as Japan and South Korea maintain stability and maintain economic growth in the process of industrialization (Ho 2001; McBeath 1998; Zeigler 1988). For this reason, in the 1990s, corporatism also became an important theoretical tool for analyzing the relationship between the state and society in China.

Jonathan Unger and Anita Chan are important advocates of using corporatism to analyze Chinese social organizations. Contrary to the newly industrialized countries in East Asia strengthening the state's control over the economy and society, China has directly or indirectly established many intermediary organizations in the form of corporatism, which were registered with government departments at all levels as well as subject to government supervision, and took on a large number of functions below the government, which in turn allowed the state to relax its control over the market and society, indicating a shift from a planned economic system to an agent-led model (Unger and Chan 1995). Unger believes that both civil society and corporatism focus on the social organization between the state and society, but different from the perspective of civil society, corporatism starts from the perspective of the state and connects with selected associations to achieve the self-purpose of the government. The selected associations serve as a bridge and a medium between the state and society and are an important mechanism for the party and the state to connect the market and society. These chambers of commerce must be officially registered and only one can be established in the same administrative area with the same or similar business scope, an institutional arrangement known as "corporatism" (Unger 1996; Unger and Chan 1996). And state corporatism is a variant of corporatism, under which state control over associations can make associations a potential tool, so that civil society cannot function effectively independently of the state (Unger 2008). Through the investigation of the three associations established by large, medium, and small business owners in Beijing, Unger further found that state corporatism plays different roles, and the government needs to redo the control of the association members it is concerned about, which led to different changes in the functioning of the three associations (Unger 2008). Having studied the trade associations and chambers of commerce composed of Chinese private entrepreneurs, Zhongpu Di also agreed with China's state corporatism, and believed that "the trade associations and chambers of commerce do not have complete autonomy but are deeply embedded in the country. The state can manipulate and control the day-to-day activities, personnel and finances of trade associations and chambers of commerce" (Dickson 2000, 2008). Margaret Pearson also believes that although industry associations become government assistants in economic and social activities, they also have their independence, which shows the duality (Janus Face) of state control and association autonomy. State control is reflected in industry associations. The establishment, personnel, and legitimacy of the industry are all affected by the government, but industry associations have the independence to express their own interests and influence the government. To indicate that it is in a socialist country and not in other capitalist countries or countries with authoritarian regimes, it is classified as "Socialist corporatism" (Pearson 1994). Zhongpu Di pointed out that the "Regulations on the Registration and Administration of Social Organizations" formulated in 1989 and revised in 1998 embodies the corporatism intention of the Chinese government, which is embodied in the regulations, that is, in different fields, the state only recognizes one organization. As the only representative of interests in this field, the state intervenes to a certain extent in its leadership election and interest demands (Dickson 2008). Recently, Unger and Chan further researched and pointed out that the Chinese government has adopted a stricter state corporatism control method on industry associations and chambers of commerce by interfering with its own interests (Unger and Chan 2015).

However, some scholars have found from the research of industry associations and chambers of commerce that corporatism is not suitable for explaining China. Jianmin Ye started from the interaction between the grassroots government and commercial organizations in a city in Shandong. He pointed out that, on the one hand, commercial organizations basically perform top-down functions, more like vassals of the state; on the other hand, social forces themselves lack internal consistency, and business organizations are only tools of individual entrepreneurs rather than associations that aggregate the demands of groups. Although the state tries to achieve social interest aggregation through social organizations, this is not an approach in the sense of corporatism (Yep 2000). Scott Kennedy believes that Chinese chambers of commerce have not really realized the characteristics of corporatism such as mandatory membership, hierarchical system and monopoly power in practice, and there is often overlap and competition among chambers of commerce, which does not meet the strict requirements of the characteristics of corporatism (Kennedy 2005). White and others also believe that corporatism is not the core goal of China's progressive reforms, and that political elites have not made efforts to build corporatism in a systematic, consistent, and clear-minded manner, and the special feature of "integration". Signs are only one aspect of the process of reconstructing complex state–society relations (White et al. 1996). Scholars seem to agree that China's regulatory framework for trade associations and chambers of commerce may have corporatist features, but the practice of Chinese trade associations and chambers of commerce does not reflect the applicability of corporatism theory in China (Howell 2012).

2.1.3 Deficiencies and Flaws in the Structural Debate

Although the research paths of pluralism theory and corporatism theory are completely different, their conclusions have something in common, that is, there is interweaving and interaction between the contemporary Chinese government and industry associations and chambers of commerce. This is reflected by the fact that industry associations and chambers of commerce do not have complete autonomy, and that the government does not fully control the operation and development of industry associations and chambers of commerce. On the contrary, the two are mutually influenced and inlaid. As a static structural analysis, the structural debate can only show readers the macroscopic picture of the relationship between the contemporary Chinese government and industry associations and chambers of commerce but cannot present the interaction between the government and industry associations and chambers of commerce, and thus cannot accurately grasp the nature of state–society relationships in contemporary China. The contemporary Chinese industry associations and chambers of commerce in the transition period are quite different in terms of regions, time, and administrative levels. In the rapidly changing China, the research description of any period may only outline the starting point rather than the ending point of analyzing the whole of China. The country itself is not monolithic. There are disputes of different interests between the central government and local governments and between government departments.

Compared with the idealized and static nature of pluralism theory and corporatism theory, China's reality is more complex. Perhaps the above theories can help us to analyze and compare, but China's state–society relationship can by no means be explained by any one theory. As Kennedy pointed out, there is no inherent label, whether it be Pluralism, Corporatism, or Deliberative Authoritarianism, that can fully reflect the nature of contemporary Chinese state–society relations (Kennedy 2008). Therefore, the emergence and development of trade associations and chambers of commerce is neither the embodiment of non-corporatism nor the formation of pluralism, but the dynamic result of the interactive reconstruction of the relationship between the state and society. In this context, analyzing the actions of trade associations and chambers of commerce in the state–society interaction is a more complex undertaking. It is even more important to put a structural theoretical label on it.

2.2 *Action Analysis of Contemporary Chinese Industry Associations and Chambers of Commerce Research*

Whether it is state–society separation or state–society cooperation, civil society and corporatism focus on static structural debates on state–society relations. With the transformation and rapid development of China's economy and society, the static structure debate has been unable to accurately reflect the diversification and dynamics of contemporary Chinese state–society relations. As Joel s. Migdal put forward "state in society" (Migdal 2001), Peter B. Evans put forward "Embedded Autonomy" (Evans 1995) and "co-governance between state and society" (Evans 1997). These theories believe that the state and society are mutually shaped and intertwined in a dynamic relationship. In this regard, researchers propose that it is not only necessary to pay attention to the relationship between state and society in China in the one-way static structure, but also to the dynamic process between the Chinese state and society, and more importantly, to the specific actions of social organizations in a specific institutional environment, their own organization and operation, and the achievements of autonomous power (Ma 2002; Pei 1998).

2.2.1 *Theoretical Exploration of Action Analysis*

Existing studies have found that the relationship between the state and society in China is an interpenetrating relationship, rather than the state in the traditional sense completely controlling the society, nor the society directly opposing the state, but "embedded activism" (Foster 2002; Ho and Edmonds 2007). Xu Huiwen proposed that the research perspective should focus on "the interaction between the state and society as conditions for each other" (Shue 2008); Richard Baum and Alexei Shevchenko pointed out that "the mutual adjustment of the state and society is at the core of China's political experience after the reform and opening up" (Baum Shevchenko 1999). Faced with the differences and diversity between industry associations, chambers of commerce, and the government, scholars try to construct a new research model to interpret the differentiated behaviors of industry associations and chambers.

Kennedy believes that the research perspective should be shifted from the theoretical debate of corporatism and civil society to the different ways in which the government and industry associations interact and the reasons for their different outcomes. Taking the lobbying of industry associations in China's steel, electronics, and software industries as an example, he believes that the different economic environments of the industries in which enterprises operate, as well as the form and scale of property rights of different enterprises are the decisive factors for the relationship between the government and industry associations (Kennedy 2005). Both the "Self-interested Bureaucratic Competition Model" and the "Fragmented Governance Structure" try to interpret it from the perspective of vertical and horizontal interest division within the country. They both believe that the Chinese state is not monolithic, and that all state departments and local governments are individuals seeking to maximize their own interests trying to maintain or compete for corresponding power and interests by forming a "symbiotic" structure with social organizations (Spires 2011; Wang 2006). In this regard, Kennedy took the government's attempt to establish China's market economy through industry associations and chambers of commerce as an example and found that industry associations and chambers of commerce used the conflict of interest and authority among state departments to gain support from different government departments (Kennedy 2008). The concept of "interest fit" is developed from the perspective of the state's strategic choice and low degree of institutionalization in handling relations with social organizations. It is verified by comparative cases of industry organization policy participation. It believes that the degree of fit between the state and social interests determines whether the state chooses to support or restrict social organizations, which is related to the state's dominance and higher discretion in the transitional period (Jiang et al. 2011). The theory of "Chinese social organizations growing through participation" is based on the self-governance of social organizations and the perspective of participating in public governance, based on the research of Zhejiang Wenzhou Chamber of Commerce, this theory breaks through the "top-down" and "bottom-up" of the development path of civil society, and no longer tortures the autonomy and mosaicism of the chamber of commerce. Rather, it strives to explore how to promote the establishment of a cooperative and co-governance relationship between the government and chambers of commerce and believes that only through extensive participation in industry governance and social management and higher governance performance, chambers of commerce can achieve greater space for legitimacy, and then expand the space for autonomy (Yu and Zhou 2013; Yu et al. 2008).

2.2.2 *Inadequacies and Shortcomings of Action Analysis*

The above-mentioned research theories or models on the diversification and dynamics of government and industry associations and chambers of commerce have broken through the static structure of the relationship between the state and society and show the complexity of the operation of industry associations and chambers of commerce. However, the theoretical exploration of the above action analysis either emphasizes the strategic behaviors caused by the government's dominance, infiltration, and control, or emphasizes the strategic actions taken by industry associations and chambers of commerce in response to different interests between governments, and the participation of industry associations and chambers of commerce in the realization of co-governance, which often ignores that the actions of the government and industry associations and chambers of commerce are the result of continuous adjustment in interaction, and this interaction is not fixed or determined by a certain force. The strategic actions of industry associations and chambers of commerce and the government's proactive response cannot be ignored. At the same time, the action analysis also ignores the influence of the incentive mechanism and restraint mechanism of different external environments on behavior subjects.

In addition, the above-mentioned research theories of action analysis tend to prefer case study analysis, and their scope of application is limited, and their explanatory power is greatly limited. Therefore, although action analysis makes up for the static and singularity of structural debates and vividly depicts the real picture of the pluralism and dynamism of the relationship between the state and society in contemporary China, it still lacks a mature theoretical analysis framework to comprehensively understand the continuous dynamic evolution logic of industry associations, chambers of commerce and government behavior on the basis of empirical research that explains. This requires us to seek the inherent common logic from the diversified actions of industry associations, chambers of commerce, and the government, and then to grasp the research on the behavior of industry associations, chambers of commerce, and the government in general. This needs us to consider the variability and uncertainty of government policies at all levels, as well as the activism of actors as well.

2.3 *Beyond Structural Debate and Action Analysis: Strategic Interactions in a Changing External Environment*

Structural Debate and Action Analysis, although complementary to each other, only reflect two aspects of contemporary Chinese industry associations and chambers of commerce research. Structural debates emphasize the structural tension and binary separation of power allocations between government and industry associations and chambers of commerce. However, the relationship between the state and society in contemporary China is not just a structural feature of society being independent of the state. Action analysis, on the other hand, observes the contribution of the actions and motivations of the agents to the interaction between the state and society from the micro level, but this does not mean that the external loop of the incentive mechanism and constraint mechanism formed by the macro structure can be ignored. The complex and changeable system faced by different agents and the complexity of the adjustment behaviors caused by other agents cannot be ignored either. Moreover, such agent analyses are best done through case studies, so the scope of research is limited, and the explanatory power is still insufficient. In other words, the macro theory of structural debate appears static and rigid, ignoring the dynamic construction of the state and social subjects; the micro theory of dynamic analysis appears fragmented, ignoring the influence of the macro-external environment. This means that existing theories cannot explain and analyze the multiplicity and dynamics of contemporary Chinese state–society relations.

The structuring theory of Anthony Giddens pointed out that social structure not only restricts human action, but also acts as a precondition and mediator for action, which makes action possible; the action of actors not only maintains the structure, but also changes the structure (Giddens 1998). This interdependent and mutually dialectical relationship between structure and dynamism is also reflected in the relationship between industry associations, chambers of commerce, and the government, reflecting the unity of structure and dynamism in contemporary Chinese state–society relations. Further, under the existing institutional environment, the government and industry associations and chambers of commerce have shown a complex situation of dual initiative of government regulation and industry associations and chambers of commerce, and this complex situation is reflected in the continuous negotiation between social organizations and the state (Saich 2000). In this way, research on the relationship between the government and industry associations and chambers of commerce should not only focus on the unity of structural agency, but also examine the strategic interaction behavior of different agencies, also known as "adaptive cooperation" (Yu and Shen 2017).

In specific research fields, research on contemporary Chinese policy formulation has always been an important position for scholars to examine the relationship between the state and society in contemporary China. From the "fragmentation" of power within a closed decision-making system described by the theory of "fragmented authoritarianism" (Lampton 1987; Lieberthal and Lampton 1992) to the theory of "fragmented authoritarianism 2.0″, the process of civic action intervening policy by environmental NGOs and the media (Mertha 2008, 2009) presents a new situation in which the relationship between the state and society in contemporary China is transformed from singularity to pluralism. Taking the policy participation of industry associations and chambers of commerce as the research object, this book focuses on the strategic interaction between the government and industry associations and chambers of commerce under the influence of the external environment from the perspective of structure–function unity, in order to interpret the diversity of the interaction between industry associations, chambers of commerce and the government.

3 Industry Associations and Chambers of Commerce Policy Participation Research

The participation of industry organizations in policy activities as a proxy for business interests became important early in the writings of pressure group theorists in the United States in the 1960s and 1970s (Lowi 1979; McConnell 1966). John W. Kingdon viewed policy-making as a series of processes of agenda setting, alternatives, and choice and decision execution. In this series of processes, policy agenda setting, decision-making, and implementation are three different levels. Correspondingly, some scholars divide the policy participation of industry associations and chambers of commerce into three categories: "policy agenda setting", "participation in decision-making", and "private benefit government". "Policy agenda setting" emphasizes the influence of industry associations and chambers of commerce outside the policy process; "participation in decision-making" refers to industry associations and chambers of commerce participating in the formulation and implementation of policies in a manner publicly recognized by the state; "private benefit government" refers to industry associations and chambers of commerce undertaking quasi-public functions transferred by government (Coleman 1985; Garrity Picard 1991).

3.1 Research on Policy Participation of Foreign Industry Associations and Chambers of Commerce

3.1.1 Policy Participation Methods of Foreign Industry Associations and Chambers of Commerce Under Different Models

Generally speaking, industry associations and chambers of commerce around the world are divided into three categories: the Continental model, the Anglo-American model, and the Hybrid model (Pu 2010). Among them, the Continental Model Chamber of Commerce, with a public law legal person established in accordance with the civil law system, implements the principle of membership obligations and mandatory people's associations. The Chamber of Commerce also undertakes government administrative functions and even has greater administrative power. The Anglo-American model, with a private law legal person, is free to withdraw, and its functions and activities are determined by the chamber of commerce. The chamber of commerce in Hybrid mode, also with a public law legal person, is free to join. At the same time, the Chamber of Commerce also undertakes part of the functions transferred by the government. Due to the different modes of trade associations and chambers of commerce in various countries, there are also certain differences in the way of policy participation of trade associations and chambers of commerce in various countries.

(1) Policy participation of industry associations and chambers of commerce in the continental model. In the continental model, German and French trade associations and chambers of commerce policy participate in a continuous dialogue channel that influences government policy. Not only the chamber of commerce of industry associations should feedback members' policy opinions and policy interests to the government, but also the German and French governments have the responsibility and obligation to consult the chamber of commerce of industry associations on the possible

impact of policy drafts and regulations on members (Pilgrim and Bonn 1995). In addition, German and French trade associations and chambers of commerce enhance their policy influence by organizing surveys and conference discussions.

(2) Policy participation of industry associations and chambers of commerce in the Anglo-American model. Under the Anglo-American model, the U.S. industry associations and chambers of commerce are mainly autonomous, and the relationship between chambers of commerce at all levels and the government is mostly a voluntary partnership, and is not required to perform some government functions. Unlike the industry associations and chambers of commerce in Germany and France, the associations don't have the Privileged Access to the Government. Like other interest groups, the U.S. Chamber of Commerce acts as the Third Pillar of power to lobby for national policy-making (Mitchell 1997). This is mainly manifested in the following two aspects: one is the direct lobbying actions of chamber of commerce staff, such as chamber representatives directly contacting parliamentarians or government officials; the other is Grassroots Advocacy, including letter writing, telephone publicity, and inviting members to participate in seminars, the purpose of which is to mobilize members to support the lobbying activities of the Chamber of Commerce (Pilgrim and Bonn 1995).

(3) Policy participation of industry associations and chambers of commerce in the hybrid model. Under the hybrid model, the Chamber of Commerce of Japan's trade associations is also an influential policy lobbying organization and maintains a close relationship with the government. Like the industry association chamber of commerce under the Continental model, the industry association chamber of commerce in Japan has the responsibility to express its own opinions on legislation and administration, which is usually achieved by: first, compiling statistical data and conducting research studies on different business policy matters; second, nominate representatives to participate in policy discussions on government committees and provide policy advice. In addition, Japanese industry associations and chambers of commerce often express their opinions through lobbying activities such as regularly organizing press conferences, publishing news magazines, issuing communiques, circulars, and leaflets (Pilgrim and Bonn 1995).

In general, the policy participation of industry associations and chambers of commerce under the Continental model shows more of the role of "participation in decision-making"; the policy participation of industry associations and chambers of commerce under the Anglo-American model is more expressed as "policy advocacy" lobbying behavior; the policy participation of industry associations and chambers of commerce under the "Hybrid model" has the characteristics of both the above-mentioned aspects.

3.1.2 State–Society Relations and Policy Participation of Foreign Industry Associations and Chambers of Commerce

Since the 1980s, there has been an upsurge in research on the role of trade associations and chambers of commerce in the political development of Western countries (Coleman and Grant 1984, 1988; Coleman 1988, 1990; Jacek 1986; Schmitter and Streeck 1999; Streeck 1983). Existing research has found that under different models, the ways of participating in policies of industry associations and chambers of commerce in various countries are not completely separated. Chambers of commerce are surpassing the role advocated by traditional policies in the political process and are beginning to undertake more quasi-public functions, including corporate coordination, private benefit government, and even to varying degrees, undertaking the public power transferred by the government (Bell 1995). Therefore, in the study of chambers of commerce in the Western academic circles, there are traditional chambers of commerce policy advocacy or lobbying roles, chambers of commerce participating in the formulation and implementation of public policies undertaking quasi-public functions. The former is more common in classic pluralism literature, while the latter appears in corporatism literature (Crouch 1983; Jacek 1986; Schmitter and Streeck 1999; Streeck 1983; Streeck and Schmitter 1985).

Some scholars also regard the coexistence of policy advocacy and participation in decision-making and implementation of the Chamber of Commerce as the debate and coordination of pluralism and corporatism. Henry J. Jacek pointed out through his research on the Canadian Chamber of Commerce that political scientists who view the Chamber of Commerce simply as a pressure group or a lobbying organization have overlooked that many important activities of the Chamber of Commerce not only promote and safeguard the interests of its members—manifesting the aspect of pluralism—but also helps the country achieve the goal of governing society—showing the trend of corporatism. Thus, the balance and adjustment of corporatism and pluralism is achieved (Jacek 1986). Using the conceptual framework of "Neo-Corporatism", Michele Garrity and Louis A. Picard analyzed the public policy formulation and implementation of trade associations and chambers of commerce from the perspective of structure and process. They consider policy participation of trade associations and chambers of commerce as a "Continuum",[1] on which one end is the role of policy advocacy or lobbying and the other end is the role of "private benefit government" that undertakes quasi-public functions, and in the middle is the process of industry associations and chambers of commerce infiltrating and influencing policy through negotiation and negotiation with the government (Garrity and Picard 1991). The changes in the policy participation of foreign trade associations and chambers of commerce reflect the interaction and changes in the relationship between the state and society.

On the analysis of the reasons for the changes in the policy participation of foreign trade associations and chambers of commerce, it has been argued that the fragmentation of the political behavior of chambers of commerce in public policy formulation and implementation alongside policy advocacy is a result of the macro-policy structure shaped by a country's national structure, fragmented economy, and business culture characteristics (Banting 1986; Bell 1995). At the same time, the governance capacity and organizational characteristics of the chamber of commerce will also have an impact on the political behavior of the chamber of commerce (Coleman and Grant 1984, 1988).

Due to the particularity and variability of the transition period, the scholars have not yet reached a conclusion on the model of Chinese industry associations and chambers of commerce, so it is impossible to copy the theory and practice of foreign industry associations and chambers of commerce policy participation (Pu 2005; Zhu 2006). However, the coexistence and integration of "policy advocacy", "participation in decision-making", and "private benefit government" in the policy participation research of foreign trade associations and chambers of commerce provide a reference for the research on policy participation of Chinese trade associations and chambers of commerce (Zhang and Jiang 2012). The analysis of the influencing factors of the macro-policy structure and

[1] The concept of "corporatism" here was originally given by Philipe C. Schmitter (1974).

the governance capacity and organizational characteristics of the chamber of commerce on the policy participation of the chamber of commerce also provides important support for the analysis of the policy participation of the chamber of commerce in my country's industry associations. Regrettably, previous studies by foreign trade associations and chambers of commerce have failed to make a dynamic analysis of the continuous adaptive behavior of both the government and the chamber of commerce during the policy participation process of trade associations and chambers of commerce under the macro-policy structure. This will be the focus of this book.

3.2 *Policy Participation Research of Domestic Industry Associations and Chambers of Commerce*

3.2.1 *System and Practice of Policy Participation of Domestic Industry Associations and Chambers of Commerce*

Compared with the West, contemporary Chinese industry associations and chambers of commerce policy participation research is in its infancy, both in theory and in practice. At the macro-policy level, in 2017, the report of the 19th National Congress of the Communist Party of China proposed that it is necessary to promote the extensive, multi-layered, and institutionalized development of consultative democracy, and to promote the consultation of social organizations, which provides a guarantee for broad, continuous, and deep policy participation. In terms of institutional text, as early as in 1999, the State Economic and Trade Commission issued a notice on "Several Opinions on Accelerating the Cultivation and Development of Associations in the Field of Industry and Commerce",[2] which required industry associations and chambers of commerce to "carry out research on industry and regional economic development and propose relevant economic policies, legislative opinions and suggestions", to "participate in the formulation of industry plans with the authorization and entrustment of government departments", to "conduct preliminary demonstrations of major technological transformation, technology introduction, investment and development projects in the industry", and to "participate in the formulation and revision of

[2] Several Opinions on Accelerating the Cultivation and Development of Associations in the Field of Industry and Commerce (for Trial Implementation), National Economic and Trade Industry [1999] No. 1016, October 22, 1999.

national standards. In 2007, the General Office of the State Council issued a programmatic document to promote the reform and development of industry associations, namely, “Several Opinions on Accelerating the Reform and Development of Industry Associations and Chambers of Commerce” (General Office of the State Council [2007] No. 36)”, which expresses the most comprehensive and clear statement of the functions of industry associations participating in policy formulation. “Before introducing major policies and measures related to the development of the industry, People’s governments at all levels should actively listen to and solicit the opinions and suggestions of the relevant industry associations. Industry associations should actively propose industry development and legislation and other aspects of the proposal, and actively participate in the research and formulation of laws and regulations, macro-control and industrial policies, participate in the formulation and revision of industry standards, industry development plans, and industry qualifications, improve industry management, and promote industry development”[3] as much as possible. The text of the management system provides legitimacy for the practical behavior of industry associations and chambers of commerce to influence policies, but the provisions on the content and behavior of industry associations and chambers of commerce policy participation are too general.

In practice, the policy participation of Chinese industry associations and chambers of commerce is mainly reflected in the following aspects: First, it undertakes government functions and participates in formulating industry standards and industry development plans. For example, Zhejiang Leather Industry Association formulated the "Twelfth Five-Year Development Plan for Zhejiang Leather Industry" and different leather product standards in 2010. Zhejiang Software Industry Association put forward industrial planning and policy suggestions to the government according to the characteristics of industrial development, and it is necessary to carry out the standard review work of "Double Soft Certification" delegated by the government (Yu et al. 2011). The second is to carry out policy advocacy and influence government decision-making. For example, since 2010, Zhejiang Semiconductor Industry Association has joined forces with Shanghai, Jiangsu and other semiconductor companies to

[3] Several Opinions on Accelerating the Reform and Development of Industry Associations and Chambers of Commerce, Guoban Fa [2007] No. 36, May 13, 2007.

submit the "Emergency Report Requesting the Continued Implementation of the Preferential Provisions of the State Council [2000] No. 18 Document" to the party and state leaders and relevant state ministries and commissions for three consecutive years, and later, together with the National Semiconductor Industry Association and some provincial and municipal semiconductor industry associations, presented Vice Premier Li Keqiang of the State Council suggestions on policies to support the integrated circuit industry (Yu et al. 2011). The third is to participate in and influence the formation and implementation of policies. For example, in the 2002 express delivery storm and the revision of the Postal Law, China International Freight Forwarders Association actively participated in policies in the process of regulating and adjusting the express delivery industry, effectively resisting the policy intention of the State Post Bureau to monopolize the industry (Li and Zeng 2006).

3.2.2 Theoretical Research on the Policy Participation of Domestic Industry Associations and Chambers of Commerce

In terms of theoretical research, the current research on the policy participation of Chinese industry associations and chambers of commerce is roughly divided into the following aspects: research on the current situation and influencing factors of policy participation in industry associations and chambers of commerce, research on the goals and methods of policy participation in industry associations and chambers of commerce, etc.

(1) The current situation of policy participation in industry associations and chambers of commerce. Existing studies have described the overall status of policy participation of Chinese industry associations and chambers of commerce. For example, Kennedy and Guosheng Deng took national industry associations as the research object and found that 89% of national industry associations "strongly agree" or "mostly agree" that "Associations should often participate in the formulation of government policies", but in practice, the proportion of associations that adopt an active policy participation strategy is only around 70%, which is much lower than the proportion of associations that "strongly agree" or "mostly agree" with the policy participation function.

(2) The factors influencing the policy participation of industry associations and chambers of commerce. Some scholars have discussed

the influencing factors of the policy participation of industry associations and chambers of commerce, mainly the government's management system arrangements for industry associations and the organizational structure attributes and autonomy of industry associations and chambers of commerce. Kennedy and Guosheng Deng point out that the time of establishment, lobbying attitude, autonomy, and representativeness of the trade association will affect the enthusiasm of the lobbying behavior of industry associations (Kennedy, Guosheng Deng 2012); Hua Jiang and Bin believe that there is a direct relationship among the regional economic development model and the formation method of industry associations, the governance structure of industry associations and the level of industry associations influencing policies (Jiang and He 2012); Dan Pan also believes that factors such as the governance capacity of industry organizations, the governance concept of government departments, and the system construction of the interaction process between the two parties affect the level of policy participation of industry organizations through the inspection of Wenzhou industry organizations (Pan 2011).

(3) Research on the goals and methods of policy participation in industry associations and chambers of commerce. Some scholars described the goals and methods of policy advocacy by industry associations and chambers of commerce. They think that in terms of policy advocacy goals, the people's congresses, CPPCC, party committees, and governments at all levels are the policy advocacy goals of industry associations and chambers of commerce; in terms of policy participation, industry associations and chambers of commerce pass policy proposals through hearings, symposiums, tea parties, research meetings, etc., and publicizing policy recommendations to the society and media to indirectly influence decision-making. Other specific practices include convening seminars or forums, organizing expert validation sessions, publishing reports jointly with specialized agencies or experts, contacting government officials through personal relationship networks, and public welfare or charitable donations (Kennedy 2009; Zhou 2009).

Overall, there is scant research on the policy participation of Chinese industry associations and chambers of commerce, nor is it sufficiently in-depth. The existing research on the policy participation of industry associations and chambers of commerce mainly has the following problems: (1) **Concepts.** The concept definition is not clear. The research on policy participation of Chinese industry associations and chambers of commerce has not yet unified the concept of policy participation, and there is confusion in the use of concepts such as policy advocacy, lobbying, and policy participation. (2) Research. The research content is still shallow. The research on the policy participation of Chinese industry associations and chambers of commerce is mainly reflected in the status quo, goals and methods, reasons, and problems. (3) The direction of research. Further research not only needs to explore the behavioral motivations, policy windows, policy entrepreneurs, and benefit coordination and distribution of policy participation of different industry associations and chambers of commerce from an internal perspective, but also needs to examine the environmental differences caused by diversified government structure, economic structure, and policy stage of different industry associations and chambers of commerce.

Based on the theoretical research and institutional practice of the policy participation of domestic and foreign industry associations and chambers of commerce, the research on policy participation of contemporary Chinese industry associations and chambers of commerce needs to explore different modes of policy participation of industry associations and chambers of commerce, which are intertwined between the macro-external environment of policy participation and the initiative of industry associations and chambers of commerce and interaction mechanism; under the framework of structure-active unity, this paper analyzes the dual initiative and strategic interaction between the government and industry associations and chambers of commerce in the policy participation of contemporary Chinese industry associations and chambers of commerce.

4 A Brief Review of Existing Research

The scholarly research on the relationship between the state and society in contemporary China has tracked the transition from the "state and society dichotomy" to "state and society interaction". In this context, the research of contemporary Chinese industry associations and chambers of commerce is examined in structural debates and action analyses, which have yielded many constructive opinions and viewpoints. However, when it comes to solving the issue of "how does the interaction between industry associations, chambers of commerce and the government show the characteristics of diversification and dynamism", the existing research results are insufficient, the macro theory of the structural debate is static and rigid, and the micro theory of action analysis is fragmented.

To sum up, the existing research needs to be advanced in the following aspects.

First, although scholars have carried out accurate analyses of the government's classified control behavior and the strategic behavior of industry associations and chambers of commerce, they have not paid attention to the government's adaptive behaviors when it is confronted with the strategic actions of industry associations and chambers of commerce. In the existing research, the active adjustment of associations and chambers of commerce has been widely recognized, but the government's active adjustment and strategic response are rarely discussed in detail by scholars. Scholars mostly explain the adjustment of party agency from the perspective of political party regime survival and the persistence of the state system, but seldom do detailed research on government agency, strategic behavior, and its changes from the perspective of the interaction between industry associations, chambers of commerce, and the government.

Second, due to the lack of attention to the adjustment of government initiative, existing research has ignored the continuity and dynamics of the interaction between industry associations and chambers of commerce and the government, so it is impossible to accurately grasp the internal evolution logic of the continuous dynamics between the government and industry associations and chambers of commerce. Relevant research focuses more on the unilateral and specific strategic actions taken by industry associations and chambers of commerce to mobilize government resources and obtain legitimacy, few discuss the dynamic mechanism of the continuous game between the government and industry associations and chambers of commerce. Put another way, the existing research has not yet made an accurate generalization of the dynamic mechanism of the interaction between industry associations, chambers of commerce, and the government.

Third, existing studies have found that different external environments have different regulatory effects on the initiative of industry associations, chambers of commerce, and the government, but they fail to realize that the interaction between industry associations, chambers of commerce, and the government also has a shaping effect on the external environment. In fact, scholars are generally worried that the existing external environment restricts the dynamic development of industry associations and chambers of commerce, so they call on the government to eliminate the obstructive systems and institutions that hinder the development of industry associations and chambers of commerce. However, scholars have failed to notice that the change in the external environment is also the result of the interaction between industry associations, chambers of commerce, and the government.

In view of this, this book argues that the reason for the diversity and dynamics of state–society interactions in contemporary China is the strategic interactions between state and society in a changing environment. Taking the policy participation of industry associations and chambers of commerce as the research carrier, this book proposes a new framework of "strategic interaction between industry associations, chambers of commerce and government in a changing environment" to make up for the shortcomings of existing research. The specific content of this study is summarized as follows:

First, it defines the initiative of the government and industry associations and chambers of commerce and carries out research on dual active subjects. The study will characterize the relationship between the contemporary Chinese government and industry associations and chambers of commerce, and offer insights into the government and industry. The factual description of the initiative behaviors requires defining the specific connotation of the initiative of the government and industry associations and chambers of commerce and exploring the behavioral logic behind the dual initiative. On this basis, the strategic interaction mechanism between the government and industry associations and chambers of commerce has the basis of action subjects.

Second, it examines the strategic interaction between the government and industry associations and chambers of commerce, and systematically analyzes the interaction mechanism between the government and industry associations and chambers of commerce. The strategic interaction research between the government and industry associations and chambers of commerce aims to solve the problems of simplification, static and fragmentation of the research on the relationship between the government and industry associations and chambers of commerce, and to break through the limitation of thinking dominated by a single force in the research on the relationship between the government and industry associations and chambers of commerce. This requires statistical analysis and case studies to describe, verify, and explore the dual adaptive behavior of the government and industry associations and chambers of commerce and the benign interaction mechanisms involved. More importantly, by examining the dynamic game process of the interaction between industry associations, chambers of commerce, and the government, we can discover the continuous and dynamic evolution logic inherent in the behavior of industry associations, chambers of commerce, and the government, and then seek the logic of the diversified interactive actions of industry associations, chambers of commerce, and the government, in order to grasp the dynamic relationship between the government and industry associations and chambers of commerce.

Finally, the current research studies the mutual shaping between the external environment and strategic interactions. After examining the strategic interaction between the government and industry associations and chambers of commerce, it is necessary to shift the research perspective to the mutual shaping process of the external environment and the strategic interaction between the government and industry associations and chambers of commerce. This requires not only paying attention to the stipulation or promotion of the external environment on the strategic interaction between the government and industry associations and chambers of commerce in the dynamic process, but also discovering the shaping effect of the dual subjects on the external environment in the strategic interaction. Capturing the mutual shaping between this external environment and strategic interaction requires showing its dynamics in case studies.

References

Alexander J C. The paradoxes of civil society. International Sociology, 1997, 12(2): 115-133.

Banting K G. The State and Economic Interests. Toronto: University of Toronto Press, 1986.

Baum R, and Shevchenko A. The state of the state'. In Merle G and R M (Eds). The Paradox of China's Post-Mao Reforms. Cambridge: Harvard University Press, 1999: 333-360.

Bell S. Between the market and the state: The role of Australian business associations in public policy. Comparative Politics, 1995: 25-53.

Breslin S. Do leaders matter Chinese politics, leadership transition and the 17th Party Congress. Contemporary Politics, 2008, 14(2): 215-231.

Chirot D. The corporatist model and socialism. Theory and Society, 1980, 9(2): 363-381.

Coleman W D. Analysing the associative action of business: Policy advocacy and policy participation. Canadian Public Administration, 1985, 28(3): 413-433.

Coleman J S. Social capital in the creation of human capital. American Journal of Sociology, 1988, 94: 95-120.

Coleman W D. State traditions and comprehensive business associations: A comparative structural analysis. Political Studies, 1990, 38(2): 231-252.

Coleman W, and Grant W. Business associations and public policy: A comparison of organisational development in Britain and Canada. Journal of Public Policy, 1984, 4(3): 209-235.

Coleman W, and Grant W. The organizational cohesion and political access of business: A study of comprehensive associations. European Journal of Political Research, 1988, 16(5): 467-487.

Crouch C. Pluralism and the new corporatism: A rejoinder. Political Studies, 1983, 31(3): 452-460.

Deng Z, and Jeffrey A. The State and Civil Society: A Social Theory Approach. Beijing: Central Compilation and Translation Press, 1999.

Dickson B J. Cooperation and corporatism in China: the logic of party adaptation. Political Science Quarterly, 2000, 115(4): 517-540.

Dickson B J. Red Capitalists in China: The Party, Private Entrepreneurs, and Prospects for Political Change. Cambridge: Cambridge University Press, 2003.

Dickson B J. Wealth into Power: The Communist Party's Embrace of China's Private Sector. Cambridge: Cambridge University Press, 2008.

Duckett J. The Entrepreneurial State in China: Real Estate and Commerce Departments in Reform Era Tianjin. London and New York: Routledge, 2002.

Edwards M. Civil Society. Cambridge: Polity Press, 2004.

Evans P B. Embedded Autonomy: States and Industrial Transformation. Princeton: Princeton University Press, 1995.

Evans P B. State-society Synergy: Government and Social Capital in Development. Berkeley: University of California, 1997.

Fewsmith J. The Logic and Limits of Political Reform in China. Cambridge: Cambridge University Press, 2013.

Foster K W. Embedded within state agencies: Business associations in Yantai. The China Journal, 2002, 47: 41-65.

Garrity M, Picard L A. Organized interests, the state, and the public policy process: An assessment of Jamaican business associations. The Journal of Developing Areas, 1991, 25(3): 369-394.

Giddens A. The constitution of society Outline of the theory of structuration. Beijing: Sanlian Bookstore, 1998.

Gilley B. Paradigms of Chinese politics: Kicking society back out. Journal of Contemporary China, 2011, 20(70): 517-533.

Gu X. The existence of civil society and public space in contemporary China: A review of Western scholars' discussion. Modern China Studies, 1994, 4.

He B. The Democratisation of China. London: Routledge, 1996.

He B. The Democratic Implications of Civil Society in China. New York: Macmillan Press Ltd, 1997.

Ho P. Greening without conflict environmentalism, NGOs and civil society in China. Development and Change, 2001, 32 (5): 893-921.

Ho P, and Edmonds R. China's embedded activism: Opportunities and constraints of a social movement. New York: Routledge, 2007.

Howell J. Civil society, corporatism and capitalism in China. Journal of Comparative Asian Development, 2012, 11(2): 271-297.

Howell J. Shall we dance welfarist incorporation and the politics of state-labour NGO relations. China Quarterly, 2015, 223: 702-723.

Hsu J Y, and Hasmath R. The Chinese Corporatist State: Adaption, Survival and Resistance. New York: Routledge, 2012.

Jacek H J. Pluralist and corporatist intermediation, activities of business interest associations, and corporate profits: Some evidence from Canada. Comparative Politics, 1986, 18(4): 419-437.

Jiang H, Zhang J, and Zhou Y. Fit of interest: An analytical framework for state-society relationships in transitional China--A case study of policy engagement by industrial organizations. Sociological Study, 2011, 3: 136-152.

Jiang H, and He B. A comparative study on the policy participation of trade associations: Nanjing and Wenzhou. Journal of Zhejiang Party School C.P.C., 2012, 1: 27-36.

Jing Y. Between control and empowerment: Governmental strategies towards the development of the non-profit sector in China. Asian Studies Review, 2015, 39(4): 589-608.

Kang X, and Han H. Classification control: A study of state Society Relations in Mainland China. Sociological Study, 2005, 6: 73-89.

Kennedy S. The Business of Lobbying in China. Cambridge: Harvard University Press, 2005.

Kennedy S. The price of competition: The failed government effort to use associations to organize China ' s market economy. In Unger J (Ed). Associations and the Chinese State: Contested Spaces. Armonk-London: ME Sharpe, 2008: 149-174.

Kennedy S. Comparing formal and informal lobbying practices in China: The capital's ambivalent embrace of capitalists. China Information, 2009, 23(2): 195-222.

Kuhn T S. The Structure of Scientific Revolutions. Chicago: University of Chicago press, 1996.

Lampton D M. Policy Implementation in Post-Mao China. Berkeley: University of California Press, 1987.

Li X, and Zeng W. The influence of industry associations on policy formation: A case study of the policy participation of the China international express working committee. Journal of Chinese Academy of Governance, 2006, 3: 76-78.

Lieberthal K G. Introduction: The 'fragmented authoritarianism' model and its limitations. In Lieberthal K G, Lampton D M (Ed). Bureaucracy, Politics and Decision Making in Post-Mao China. Berkeley: University of California Press, 1992: 1-22.

Lieberthal K G, Lampton D M. Bureaucracy, Politics, and Decision Making in Post-Mao China. Berkeley: University of California Press, 1992.

Lowi T J. The End of Liberalism: The Second Republic of the United States. New York: Norton, 1979.

Ma Q. The governance of NGOs in China since 1978: How much autonomy. Nonprofit and Voluntary Sector Quarterly, 2002, 31(3): 305-328.

McBeath G A. The changing role of business associations in democratizing Taiwan. Journal of Contemporary China, 1998, 7(18): 303-320.

McConnell G. Private Power and American Democracy. New York: Knopf New York, 1966.

Mertha A. China's Water Warriors: Citizen Action and Policy Change. Ithaca: Cornell University Press, 2008.

Mertha A. "Fragmented Authoritarianism 2.0": Political pluralization in the Chinese policy process. The China Quarterly, 2009, 200: 995-1012.

Migdal J S. State in Society: Studying How State and Society Transform and Constitute One Another. Cambridge: Cambridge University Press, 2001.

Mitchell N J. The Conspicuous Corporation: Business, Public Policy, and Representative Democracy. Ann Arbor: University of Michigan Press, 1997.

Nathan A J. Authoritarian resilience. Journal of Democracy, 2003, 14(1): 6-17.

Nevitt C E. Private business associations in China: Evidence of civil society or local state power. The China Journal, 1996, 36: 25-43.

O'Brien K J, Li L. Rightful Resistance in Rural China. Cambridge and New York: Cambridge University Press, 2006.

Oi J C. The role of the local state in China' s transitional economy. The China Quarterly, 1995, 144: 1132-1149.

Pan D. The current situation and influencing factors of policy participation of industry organizations--An empirical study based on industrial organizations in Wenzhou. East China Economic Management, 2011, 11: 106-109.

Parris K. Local initiative and national reform: The Wenzhou model of development. The China Quarterly, 1993, 134: 242-263.

Pearson M M. The Janus face of business associations in China: Socialist corporatism in foreign enterprises. The Australian Journal of Chinese Affairs, 1994, 31: 25-46.
Pei M. Chinese civic associations: An empirical analysis. Modern China, 1998, 24(3): 285-318.
Perry E J. Trends in the study of Chinese politics: State-society relations. The China Quarterly, 1994, 139: 704-713.
Pilgrim M, Bonn R M. National Chambers of Commerce: Primer on the Organization and Role of Chamber Systems. Washington, D C: Center for International Private Enterprise (CIPE), 1995.
Pu W. Report on the development of Chinese chambers of commerce. Beijing: Social Sciences Academic Press, 2005.
Pu W. Research on the legislation of Chinese chamber of commerce law. Beijing: Central Compilation and Translation Press, 2010.
Saich T. Negotiating the state: The development of social organizations in China. The China Quarterly, 2000, 161: 124-141.
Schmitter P C. Still the century of corporatism. The Review of Politics, 1974, 36(1): 85-131.
Schmitter P C, and Streeck W. The Organization of business interests: Studying the associative action of business in advanced industrial societies. MPIfG Discussion Paper, 1999.
Shen Y, and Yu J. Local government and NGOs in China: Performance-based collaboration. China: An International Journal, 2017, 15(2): 177-191.
Shue V. Theory and irony in the study of contemporary China. In Shue V (Ed). The Reach of the State: Sketches of the Chinese Body Politic. Stanford: Stanford University Press, 1988: 11-29.
Shue V. Rule as repertory and the compound essence of authority. Modern China, 2008, 34(1): 141-151.
Spires A J. Contingent symbiosis and civil society in an authoritarian state: Understanding the survival of China's grassroots NGOs. American Journal of Sociology, 2011, 117(1): 1-45.
Streeck W. Between pluralism and corporatism: German business associations and the state. Journal of Public Policy, 1983, 3(3): 265-284.
Streeck W, and Schmitter P C. Community, market, state and associations? The prospective contribution of interest governance to social order. European Sociological Review, 1985, 1(2): 119-138.
Teets J C. Let many civil societies bloom: The rise of consultative authoritarianism in China. The China Quarterly, 2013, 213: 1-20.
Tsai K S. Adaptive informal institutions and endogenous institutional change in China. World Politics, 2006, 59(1): 116.

Tsai L L. Accountability without Democracy: Solidarity Groups and Public Goods Provision in Rural China. Cambridge: Cambridge University Press, 2007.

Tsang S. Consultative Leninism: China's new political framework. Journal of Contemporary China, 2009, 18(62): 865-880.

Unger J. Bridges: Private business, the Chinese government and the rise of new associations. The China Quarterly, 1996, 147: 795-819.

Unger J. Associations and the Chinese State: Contested Spaces. New York: ME Sharpe, 2008.

Unger J, and Chan A. China, corporatism, and the East Asian model. The Australian Journal of Chinese Affairs, 1995, 33: 29-53.

Unger J, and Chan A. State corporatism and business associations in China: A comparison with earlier emerging economies of East Asia. International Journal of Emerging Markets, 2015, 10(2): 178-193.

Unger J, Chan A. Corporatism in China: A developmental state in an East Asian context. In Bowles P, McCormick B L and Unger J (Eds). China After Socialism: In the Footsteps of Eastern Europe or East Asia. Armonk: ME Sharpe, 1996.

Wang H. Chinese social organizations in controversy: A perspective on the relationship between state and society. Taipei: Weber Culture International Publishing Co., 2006.

Wang S, and Song C. Independence or autonomy: Rethinking the characteristics of Chinese social organizations. Social Science in China Press, 2013, 5: 50-66.

Wank D L. Private business, bureaucracy, and political alliance in a Chinese city. The Australian Journal of Chinese Affairs, 1995, 33: 55-71.

White G. Prospects for civil society in China: A case study of Xiaoshan city. The Australian Journal of Chinese Affairs, 1993, 29: 63-87.

White G, Howell J A, and Shang X. In Search of Civil Society: Market Reform and Social Change in Contemporary China. Oxford: Clarendon Press, 1996.

White L T. Unstately Power, Volume. Local Causes of China's Intellectual, Legal, and Government Reforms. Armonk: ME Sharpe, 1998.

Wiarda H J. Corporatism and development in the Iberic-Latin world: Persistent strains and new variations. The Review of Politics, 1974, 36(1): 3-33.

Yang D. Remaking the Chinese Leviathan: Market Transition and the Politics of Governance in China. Palo Alto: Stanford University Press, 2004.

Yep R. The limitations of corporatism for understanding reforming China: An empirical analysis in a rural county. Journal of Contemporary China, 2000, 9(25): 547-566.

Yu J, Guo S. Civil Society and Governance in China. New York: Palgrave Macmillan, 2012.

Yu J, and Shen Y. Adaptive cooperation: strategic changes in the relationship between the Chinese government and social organizations since the 18th National Congress. Cass Journal of Political Science, 2017, 3: 39-41.

Yu J, Zhou J. Local governance and business associations in Wenzhou: A model for the road to civil society in China. Journal of Contemporary China, 2013, 22(81): 394-408.

Yu J, Jiang H, and Zhou J. Growing Chinese Civil society through participation: A study based on the Zhejiang Wenzhou chamber of commerce. Hangzhou: Zhejiang University Press, 2008.

Yu J, Shen Y, and Wu X. The role types of industry associations in promoting industrial upgrading and their realization mechanism. Journal of Zhejiang University (Humanities and Social Sciences), 2011, 41(6): 23-35.

Yu J, Zhou J and Jiang H. A Path for Chinese Civil Society: A Case Study on Industrial Associations in Wenzhou, China. New York: Lexington Books, 2012.

Zeigler L H. Pluralism, Corporatism, and Confucianism: Political Associations and Conflict Regulation in the United States, Europe, and Taiwan. Philadelphia: Temple University Press, 1988.

Zhang J. Business associations in China: TWO regional experiences. Journal Of Contemporary Asia, 2007, 37(2): 209-231.

Zhang J, and Jiang H. Research on policy participation of foreign industry organizations and implications for China. Social Sciences in Nanjing, 2012, 2: 80-83.

Zhang Z, and Zhuang W. Informal politics: Action strategies of a grassroots NGO--A study on the preparatory committee of the friendship association at Guangzhou owners' committee, 2008.

Zhang, J. From structural debate to action analysis: A review of overseas Chinese NGO research. Society, 2012, 32(3): 198-223.

Zhao X. Chinese NGOs' strategies towards the government: A preliminary examination. Open Times, 2004, 6: 5-23.

Zhou K X. How the Farmers Changed China: Power of the People. Boulder, CO: Westview Press, 1996.

Zhou J. Policy advocacy of industrial organizations: Current situation, problems and mechanism construction. Chinese Public Administration, 2009, 9: 91-96.

Zhou Y. State society interdependence model in market transition: A case study of the farmers' city in Wenzhou during the early reform era. Journal of Contemporary China, 2013, 22(81): 476-498.

Zhu W. The generation and development mode choice of Chinese chambers of commerce. Journal of Management World, 2006, 8: 144-145.

CHAPTER 3

Diversity and Dynamics of the Interaction Between Business Associations and the Government in China

1 A Research Analytical Framework: Strategic Interaction Between Industry Associations, Chambers of Commerce, and the Government in a Changing External Environment

This book seeks to answer the research question: "Why are the interactions between China's industry associations, chambers of commerce, and government diverse and dynamic?"

The research logic of this study requires exploration of the key factors affecting these interactions and their operating mechanisms based on the research foundation of institutional theory and resource dependence theory. For that reason, it is also necessary to examine the external environment in which the policy participation of industry associations and chambers of commerce is embedded (Pfeffer and Salancik 2003). This will necessarily include the interactive subjects and their initiatives which will clarify the specific connotations, core elements, and characteristics as they appear through the "external environment", "dual initiative", and "strategic interaction".

The focus on the "external environment" acknowledges that the behaviors of the government and industry associations and chambers of commerce are affected by the complex and changeable circumstances outside the control in which they operate. The "dual initiative" in this study accepts that both the government and industry associations are active and take actions based on their own interests and capabilities.

Y. Shen, *The Policy Participation of Business Associations in China*,
https://doi.org/10.1007/978-981-96-1096-9_3

Strategic interaction means that industry associations and chambers of commerce adopt different strategies to deal with government actions, while the government will also adjust its own behavior according to the different strategies of industry associations and chambers of commerce in effect, while the external environment restricts or constructs the initiatives of the government and industry associations and chambers of commerce, it is at the same time being shaped by these actors.

On this basis, this book seeks to clarify the specific content of the initiatives of the government as well as industry associations and chambers of commerce. What are the feasible pathways for strategic interaction? What form is the form taken by the mutual shaping of the external environment and strategic interaction?

Along with some help from institutional theory and resource dependence theory organizational analysis, it is necessary to perform an organizational analysis that examines the government as well as industry associations and chambers of commerce as individual organizations. The objective is to observe how these actors mobilize resources and initiate their strategic interactions then adjust their behavior to shape the external environment.

Institutional theoretical research has been evolving. It began with the decisive influence of institutional environment on organizational structure and activities, then moved to the impact of organizational initiatives on institutional environment, and then entered a phase of theoretical research on the interactions between institutional structures and initiatives. Early neo-institutionalist scholars tend to highlight the numerous ways institutional mechanisms constrain organizational structures and their activities. For example, John Meyer and Brian Rowan emphasize the changes in the broad and organizational activities (Meyer and Rowan 1977). Paul DiMaggio and Walter Powell distinguish between three mechanisms—coercion, imitation, normalization—that produce convergence effects among institutions in the field (Powell and DiMaggio 1983). Later research began to focus on individual and organizational innovation, strategic behavior, and how they facilitate institutional change, which is in line with DiMaggio's emphasis on the role of interests and actors in institutional theory (DiMaggio 1988). Walter Powell believes that the scope of institutional analysis needs to be expanded to study the processes that cause changes in the institutional environment (Powell 1991). Christine

Oliver discusses the potential of individuals and organizations in the institutional process to make changes in the face of institutional requirements as part of their coping strategies (Oliver 1991).

Although these works illuminate the opposing views of institutional structure and agency, they also prioritize their own research pathways. However, as Giddens' "structural" theory shows, institutional structure and agency are not opposed to each other, but interact in "the duality of social structure", a space that is both a product of social action and a platform of social action (Giddens 1998). That is to say, the proactive behavior of the government and industry associations and chambers of commerce is not only regulated by the external environment, but also constructs and shapes changes within it. As organizations, the government and industry associations and chambers of commerce will also adjust themselves due to their different strategic actions.

Resource dependence theory emphasizes that an organization needs to rely on a variety of resources to survive and develop, but the organization cannot provide these resources to maintain itself. External constraints and internal power structures form the behavioral conditions of the organization, and the organization needs to have the ability to mobilize resources and interact with the environmental elements on which it depends (Berry 2003; Pfeffer and Salancik 2003). This requires the organization to act upon its priorities, mobilize its internal and external resources, enhance the organization's mobilization will and self-capacity, and realize organizational change and environmental change through mergers, alliances, lobbying, or governance methods. For non-profit organizations, resource mobilization theory emphasizes that the policy participation of non-profit organizations is attributed to the effective drive of tangible resources such as financial resources and human resources (Cress and Snow 1996; Edwards and McCarthy 2004; McCarthy and Zald 1987). Social capital theory makes up for the deficiencies of resource mobilization theory by considering the research on the intangible resources of the resource mobilization capabilities of non-profit organization policy participation. This includes social networks based on shared rules and values, trust, and intangible resources such as the personal or organizational relationships between different actors with reciprocal interests (Coleman 1988; Portes 1998; Putnam 1995; Schneider 2009).

Thus, as an organization, the government has its own interests within the existing system. It will use incentives and constraints to mobilize the resources of business associations to serve economic growth and social stability, and then reveal its intentions as interested actors make their interests known through policy participation. Likewise, industry associations and chambers of commerce coordinate member interests and represent them through the mobilization of the government's available resources to make policy participation as effective as possible. These mobilized resources include human, financial, and other tangible resources, as well as social capital and other intangible resources. All three parties will strategically mobilize their resources to effectively use their interactions and thereby achieve their policy goals.

Combining institutional theory and resource dependence theory, this book interprets the multiple dynamic relationships between government and its industry associations as "the strategic interaction between the government and industry associations and chambers of commerce in a changing external environment", including the strategic interactions between the government and industry associations and chambers of commerce. Interactions and the mutual regulation and shaping of the external environment through strategic interactions constitute the framework of research and analysis in this book (see Fig. 1).

2 Research Hypothesis: Dual Initiative, External Environment, and Strategic Interaction

The research and analysis framework of "Strategic Interaction between the Government and Industry Associations and Chambers of Commerce under the Changing External Environment" is composed of the following research dimensions: the external environment, dual initiatives, and strategic interactions as the main research dimensions. It can be further divided into two parts: (1) the dual initiative of the government and industry associations and chambers of commerce and the impact of policy participation of industry associations and chambers of commerce; (2) the mutual regulation and shaping between the external environment and strategic interactions.

2.1 Dual Initiative and Industry Association Chamber Policy Involvement

Scholars have long suggested that the actors influencing the policy participation of social organizations in contemporary China are the social organizations themselves and the government. The dual initiative between

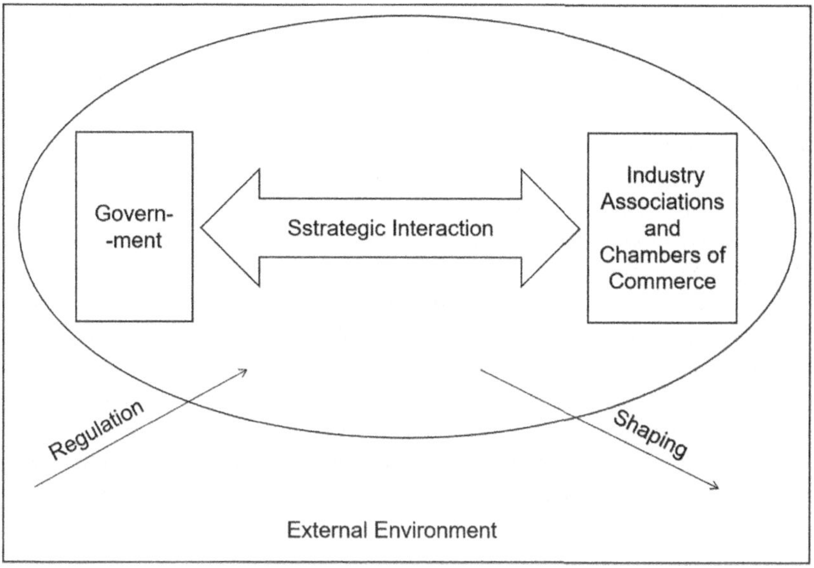

Fig. 1 Analytical framework

them is reflected in the ability of those social organizations to participate in policy and the government's policy motivations (Zhan and Jiang 2012; Zheng 2004).

For William D. Coleman, "coordination" and "autonomy" are the organizational characteristics that reflect the capabilities of trade associations and chambers of commerce's policy to advocate for their members. "Coordination" refers to their ability to coordinate complex information and needs, including the properties of the associations, such as the horizontal differentiation of products or services in specific economic fields, the vertical differences of products, service groups, and regions at different economic levels, the integration and coordination of different vertical and horizontal units, and the interests of representatives that are concentrated in a small number of industry associations and chambers of commerce where there is no competition. "Autonomy" refers to the diversification of resources, including diversity of funding sources and member support, the balances between full-time staff and member experts and between; administrators and executors, the association's self-assembled information base, and the privileges conferred on it by the state (Coleman 1985).

As a feature of the development history of China's industry associations and chambers of commerce, the ability to participate, domestic scholars believe, is an important dimension that affects the quality of their policy participation. Hua Jiang and Bin He posit that the governance structure of industry associations and chambers of commerce determines the effect of their policy advocacy (Jiang and He 2012). Kennedy and Guosheng Deng believe that an industry association's membership size, representativeness, age, and autonomy (as measured by business supervisory units) will affect its lobbying behavior. Among them, the higher the degree of representativeness of the association, the more inclined it is to actively lobby; the stronger its autonomy, the more inclined it is to actively lobby.

To sum up, the policy participation ability of an industry association or chamber of commerce includes both the structure and its willingness to act independently. These are manifested in its representativeness, autonomy, financial resources, and human resources.

Therefore, this study hypothesized the following:

Hypothesis 1 The stronger the policy participation ability of an industry association or chambers of commerce, the more policy participation it will undertake.

Hypothesis 1(a) The stronger the representativeness of an industry association or chamber of commerce the more policy participation it will undertake.

Hypothesis 1(b) The stronger the autonomy of an industry association or chamber of commerce, the more policy participation it will undertake;

Hypothesis 1(c) The more independent the financial resources of an industry association or chamber of commerce, the more policy participation it will undertake;

Hypothesis 1(d) The more independent the human resources of an industry association or chamber of commerce, the more policy participation it will undertake.

2.2 The Policy Willingness of Government and the Policy Participation of Industry Associations and Chambers of Commerce

Whether it be Civil society theory, which relies on a view of the state–society relationship as antagonistic, or corporatism, which uses institutional arrangements to explain how government dominates society, both presume government is motivated to dominate society and monopolize power. A government's policy will is the aggregate of the attitudes, motivations, and actions expressed by the government in the decision-making process. However, China's governments are far from monolithic. Between the central and local governments vertically, there are different operational logics at work, and among governmental departments horizontally, there exist conflicts of interest (Tsai 2004). Because this book focuses on the policy participation of local industry associations and chambers of commerce, it examines the sources and institutional foundations of local government policy motivations and then analyzes the relationships among them and those of industry associations and chambers of commerce.

The separation of powers between the central government and local governments has prompted local governments to play an increasingly significant role in local affairs and economic development. Scholars suggest there are many institutional foundations for local government behavioral logic: the pursuit of economic growth, the maximization of local financial benefits, and the performance evaluation of local officials and cadres (Landry 2008; Montinola, Qian and Weingast 1995; Yu and Gao 2012; Zhou 2008). Local governments adhere to the principle of not violating any central policies as a guiding principle, but they also weigh the contribution of diverse groups to their "real interests" and "social stability" to independently formulate and implement economic development policies suitable for local conditions.

Government support in transitional countries plays a vital role in the functions of industry associations and chambers of commerce. Those that receive support from government policies, funds, or functional mandates can play their roles more effectively (Jiang 2006; Yu et al. 2013). The reason the government is willing to support the development of industry associations and chambers of commerce is that they are a legitimate link between the government and industry (Unger 1996). On the one hand, as an assistant to local government, industry associations and chambers of commerce help government departments to quickly and timely understand enterprise and industry information, perform the functions of managing enterprises and markets, and provide quasi-public goods for the industry. On the other hand, industry associations and chambers of commerce help government departments to gather and transmit corporate interest demands, reduce pressure on government departments, and thus reduce social risks (Yu et al. 2004). To better promote GDP growth, to reduce enterprise dissatisfaction, and to maintain good relations between government and enterprises, local governments need industry associations and chambers of commerce to investigate and obtain industry market information and enterprise development needs when formulating and implementing industry economic development policies. Enterprises often use industry associations and chambers of commerce as channels to express their own interests to the government and thereby influence the formation of policy, particularly at the local level.

Therefore, a local government's initiatives will include government's policy will which is based on a combination of factors such as the pursuit of economic growth, the maximization of local financial benefits, the performance evaluation of local officials and cadres, and the control of political risks. The policy participation of industry associations and chambers of commerce operates and unfolds within the policy will formed by the above-mentioned multiple and intertwined motives and mechanisms of local governments. Although the government's policy will is intertwined with multiple motivations and complex mechanisms, the behaviors and performances that reflect the government's policy will are more intuitive, such as the delegation of government functions, government financial support, and the granting of priority paths for policy participation. Considering that the theme of this book focuses on the policy participation of industry associations and chambers of commerce, a government's policy will is manifest most acutely in that government's "priority path for policy participation" of the targeted industry associations and chambers of commerce.

Based on this discussion, this study posited the following:

Hypothesis 2 The greater the priority path for policy the government gives to an industry association or chamber of commerce, the more it will participate in the policy process.

3 External Environment and Strategic Interaction

Existing studies suggest that there is often competition, interactions, and power struggles between the state and society in a "specific field".[1] This perspective is of great significance for the analysis of contemporary Chinese social organizations (Ji 2013). The external environment, as an external factor affecting the behavior of the government and industry associations and chambers of commerce, has the characteristics of complex variability. In this complex, external environment, industry associations, chambers of commerce, and the government must push their own initiatives and use existing rules and resources as construction actions to engage in strategic interaction.

(1) External Environment

The external environment refers to the external factors that regulate or promote the behavior of the government and industry associations and chambers of commerce. It includes the core elements such as the macro-policy of the higher party committee or the government, market demand, and environmental differences at different policy stages.

Existing studies believe that the policy participation of industry associations and chambers of commerce is shaped by the country's national structure, economic structure, business culture, and other macro-policy structures (Banting 1986; Bell 1995).

All industry associations and chambers of commerce in China are governed within a unified macro institutional environment[2], that is explicitly mapped in the "Regulations on the Registration and Management of Social Organizations" and "Several Opinions on Accelerating the Reform and Development of Industry Associations and Chambers of

[1] "Field" means that every action of an actor is affected by the field in which the action takes place, not only the physical environment, but also the behavior of other actors and many factors connected to it. Representative research scholars include Bourdieu, Kaufka, and Lewin.

[2] Institutional environment refers to all the formal or informal norms used by the state to regulate and restrict the activities of civil organizations, including the constitution, laws, administrative regulations, party policies, and informal systems. The informal systems mean the official attitude toward NGOs and the "hidden rules" that affect the activities and functions of NGOs (Chu Songyan 2009; Yu Keping 2006).

Commerce" (General Office of the State Council [2007] No. 36), etc., and they are expected to carry out policy participation activities under laws, regulations, and policy regulations. At the same time, the macroeconomic development environment, higher-level government policies and regulations, and higher-level government leadership opinions all constitute the external environment of industry associations and chambers of commerce in policy participation. However, the external environments in which the policy participation of the industry associations and chambers of commerce are fairly different, particularly at the local level. The policy participation of each association and chamber is deeply affected by the external environments peculiar to it, and thus adds another layer of complexity and variability to the process.

Similarly, government behavior in the context of policy participation is also constrained by different external environments. On the one hand, government behavior in the context of policy participation is constrained by the policies and laws and regulations of higher-level party committees and government departments; on the other hand, government behavior in the context of policy participation is also affected by external environments such as the macroeconomic development situation, social needs, and public concerns (Huang 2017). However, the influence of the external environment varies from government to government (Huang 2015). Obviously, local governments are at different stages of development and must navigate the economic and social needs of their constituents. Likewise, policies, laws, and regulations are not uniform across the country. The degree of application in the government will also vary, which reflects the complexity and variability of the external environment in which the government acts in the context of policy participation.

(2) Strategic Interaction

In different external environments, industry associations, chambers of commerce, and the government will push their own initiatives, using existing rules and resources as an important means of constructing action strategies to carry out strategic interactions (Hildebrandt 2013). Based on the motivation theory of organizations pursuing interests and legitimacy, Oliver described five common strategic responses that individual organizations may choose in the institutional process (Oliver 1991; Scott 2010):

(1) Acquiesce (including habit, imitation, and compliance). The reason the organization adopts and implements this coping strategy may be based on single or comprehensive motivations such as enhancing legitimacy, fear of being sanctioned, and hoping to obtain additional resources; (2) Compromise, including tradeoffs, pacification, and negotiation. Organizations in multiple situations often have considerable room to operate, understand, bargain, or compromise; (3) Avoid, including concealment, buffering, and decoupling. "Decoupling" its structural features from technical activities when circumstances so require. Organizations using this strategy try to hide themselves and prevent certain parts of the organization from being affected; (4) Defy, including disbandment, challenge, and attack. When there are substantive differences between the organization that imposes the requirements of the focus organization; (5) Manipulate, including co-opt, influence, and control, where the organization cooperates with the environment purposefully, influences, or even controls the environment. Organizations protect themselves and increase their bargaining power by building relationships with significant sources of power. In addition, Scott believes that the collective coping strategies of multiple organizations have greater influence and may affect environmental requirements or the nature of pressure, and even redefine the rules and logic of operations in the field (Scott 2010). Thus, an individual organization may choose from six common strategic actions and responses in the institutional process (see Table 1).

According to Oliver and Scott's theory, trade associations, chambers of commerce, and governments in policy engagement may exhibit different strategic interactions. There are many ways in which industry associations and chambers of commerce participate in policies. For example, the "policy information transfer" behavior of industry associations and chambers of commerce may be the result of industry associations' acquiescence or compliance with policies. This is also the coping strategy adopted by most industry associations and chambers of commerce. The motivation is to strengthen the legitimacy of the organization and obtain government power resources; the "policy game or mutual benefit" behavior of industry associations and chambers of commerce may be the result of repeated negotiations between industry associations and chambers of commerce and the government.

Table 1 Strategic actions and responses in the interaction between industry associations and governments

Policy Action	*Specific Contents*	*Behavioral Motivation*	*Organization*
Acquiescence	Habit, imitation, and compliance	Increased legitimacy, fear of sanctions, hope for additional resources	Industry associations and chambers of commerce
Compromise	Tradeoffs, pacification, and negotiation	Win–win through operation or bargaining	Government; Industry associations and chambers of commerce
Avoidance	Concealment, buffering, and decoupling	Hiding and preventing certain parts of the organization from being affected	Government; Industry associations and chambers of commerce
Defy	Disband, challenge, and attack	Conflict of interests when there is substantial disagreement	Government; Industry associations and chambers of commerce
Manipulation	Co-opt, influence, and control	Self-protection and increase bargaining power by building relationships with important sources of power	Government; Industry associations and chambers of commerce
Multi-organization cooperation	Strategic alliances, partners	Through cooperation with different organizations, complement each other's advantages, share resources, and enhance resource operation capabilities	Industry associations and chambers of commerce

However, the policy participation of industry associations and chambers of commerce is a complex process: sometimes, a certain policy participation behavior is the result of continuous interaction between industry associations and chambers of commerce using different strategies, and it may also depend on the influence of different external environments. This kind of policy participation behavior is the avoidance strategies that industry association and chambers of commerce use to realize the "coupling" between structure and activities to achieve the purpose of policy participation, which is why "those seemingly independent social organizations have actual autonomy" (Lu 2007). At the same time, in the face of different strategic behaviors of industry associations and chambers of commerce, the government will also adjust its policy with regard to the external environment and its own interests. The government may adopt manipulation strategies to co-opt, influence, and control industry associations and chambers of commerce. The government may also adopt avoidance strategies to temporarily alleviate the policy demands made by the industry associations and chambers of commerce to sidestep a direct conflict.

Due to the complexity and variability of the external environment, industry associations and chambers of commerce need to adopt different strategies to deal with changes in their external environments and government policy will. Similarly, the government must also adjust its own behavior according to the different strategies of the industry associations and chambers of commerce and changes in its external environment. Therefore, the relationship between strategic interactions and the external environment is also reflected in the corresponding strategic adjustments made by the government and industry associations and chambers of commerce as their external environments change and their dynamic strategies evolve. This observation also stresses the significant role that strategic interaction plays in shaping the institutional environment, which at the end of the day turns out to be the embodiment of the logic of structural dynamic unity.

Based on this discussion, this study puts forward the following hypotheses:

Hypothesis 3 The more interaction between industry associations, chambers of commerce and the government, the more continuous and dynamic they will be.

Hypothesis 4 The more the external environment interacts with the strategic interaction, the more the two shape each other.

To sum up, under the research framework of "Strategic Interaction between the Government and Industry Associations and Chambers of Commerce under Changing External Environment", this study proposes the following four research hypotheses:

Hypothesis 1 "The stronger the ability of industry associations and chambers of commerce to participate in policies, the more the greater the policy participation of industry associations and chambers of commerce";

Hypothesis 2 "The more policy participation paths given by the government, the more industry associations and chambers of commerce participate in policies";

Hypothesis 3 "The more interactions between industry associations and chambers of commerce and the government, the more it can present continuity and dynamics";

Hypothesis 4 "The more the external environment interacts with strategic interactions, the more they can shape each other".

Among them, Hypotheses 1 and 2 were tested through large-sample statistical research; Hypotheses 3 and 4 were tested through multi-case comparative analysis.

References

Banting K G. The State and Economic Interests. Toronto: University of Toronto Press, 1986.

Bell S. Between the market and the state: The role of Australian business associations in public policy. Comparative Politics, 1995: 25-53.

Berry J M. A Voice for Nonprofits. Washinton D C: Brookings Institution Press, 2003.

Chu S. Analysis of the institutional environment for citizen participation in China. The Journal of Shanghai Administration Institute, 2009, 1: 46-56.

Coleman W D. Analysing the associative action of business: Policy advocacy and policy participation. Canadian Public Administration, 1985, 28(3): 413-433.

Coleman J S. Social capital in the creation of human capital. American Journal of Sociology, 1988, 94: 95-120.

Cress D M, and Snow D A. Mobilization at the margins: Resources, benefactors, and the viability of homeless social movement organizations. American Sociological Review, 1996, 61: 1089-1109.

DiMaggio P. Interest and agent in institutional theory. In Zucker L G (Ed). Institutional Patterns and Organizations: Culture and Environment. Cambridge, MA: Ballinger, 1988: 3-22.

Edwards B, and McCarthy J D. Resources and social movement mobilization. In The Blackwell Companion to Social Movements, 2004: 116-152.

Giddens A. The constitution of society Outline of the theory of structuration. Beijing: Sanlian Bookstore, 1998.
Hildebrandt T. Social Organizations and the Authoritarian State in China. Cambridge: Cambridge University Press, 2013.
Huang X. Institutional environment and development of social organizations in contemporary China. Social Sciences in China Press, 2015, 9: 146-164.
Huang X. Rethinking the conditions for the growth of social organizations in China: An overarching theoretical perspective. Sociological Study, 2017, 1: 101.
Ji Y. Social organization in contemporary China: theoretical perspectives and empirical research. Sociological Study, 2013, 5: 219-241.
Jiang J. Constraints on the functioning of industry associations in transitional countries: An analysis based on the government's perspective. Research Financial and Economic Issues, 2006, 11: 93-96.
Jiang H, and He B. A comparative study on the policy participation of trade associations: Nanjing and Wenzhou. Journal of Zhejiang Party School C.P.C., 2012, 1: 27-36.
Landry P F. Decentralized Authoritarianism in China. New York: Cambridge University Press, 2008.
Lu Y. The autonomy of Chinese NGOs: A new perspective. China: An International Journal, 2007, 5(2): 173-203.
McCarthy J D, and Zald M N. Resource mobilization and social movements: A partial theory. Social Movements in an Organizational Society, 1987: 15-42.
Meyer J W, and Rowan B. Institutionalized organizations: Formal structure as myth and ceremony. American Journal of Sociology, 1977: 340-363.
Montinola G, Qian Y and Weingast B R. Federalism, Chinese style: The political basis for economic success in China. World Politics, 1995, 48(1): 50-81.
Oliver C. Strategic responses to institutional processes. Academy of Management Review, 1991, 16(1): 145-179.
Pfeffer J, and Salancik G. The External Control of Organizations: A Resource Dependence Perspective. Palo Alto: Stanford University Press, 2003.
Portes A. Social capital: Its origins and applications in modern sociology. Annual Review of Sociology, 1998, 24: 1-24.
Powell W W. Expanding the scope of institutional analysis. In Powell W W and DiMaggio P J (Eds). New Institutionalism in Organizational Analysis. Chicago: University of Chicago Press, 1991: 183-203.
Powell W W, and DiMaggio P. The iron cage revisited: Institutional isomorphism and collective rationality in organizational fields. American Sociological Review, 1983, 48(2): 147-160.
Putnam R D. Bowling alone: America's declining Social Capital. Journal of Democracy, 1995, 6(1): 65-78.

Schneider J A. Organizational social capital and nonprofits. Nonprofit and Voluntary Sector Quarterly, 2009, 38 (4): 643-662.

Scott W. R. Institutions and organizations--Ideology and material Interests. Beijing: People's University of China Press, 2010.

Tsai K S. Back-Alley Banking: Private Entreprenuers in China. Ithaca: Cornell University Press, 2004.

Unger J. Bridges: Private business, the Chinese government and the rise of new associations. The China Quarterly, 1996, 147: 795-819.

Yu K. China's civil society: Concept, classification and institutional environment. Social Science in China Press, 2006, 1: 109-122.

Yu J, and Gao X. Behavioral logic and institutional basis of local developmental government. Social Science in China Press, 2012, 5: 95-112.

Yu J, Huang H, and Fang L. Between government and enterprise: a study on Wenzhou chamber of commerce. Hangzhou: Zhejiang People's Publishing House, 2004.

Yu J, Shen Y, and Zhou J. The role of government support and trade associations in Economic Transformation and Upgrading--A study based on Zhejiang Province, Jiangsu Province and Shanghai. The Journal of Shanghai Administration Institute, 2013, 2: 4-13.

Zhang J, and Jiang H. Research on policy participation of foreign industry organizations and implications for China. Social Sciences in Nanjing, 2012, 2: 80-83.

Zheng Z. Policy participation and influence patterns of Non-Governmental Organizations (NGOs). Chinese Public Administration, 2004, 5: 32-35.

Zhou L. Local government in transition: Officials' motivation and governance. Shanghai: Gezhi Publishing House, 2008.

CHAPTER 4

Research Design and Research Method

1 Research Samples and Data Sources

This book uses data derived from the "Development Database of Industry Associations and Chambers of Commerce" of the Research Center for Social Organizations and Social Governance of Zhejiang University that was collected in two stages. The first stage, from June to August 2012, included a large-sample questionnaire survey. The second stage, from March to May 2014, followed up with in-depth case interviews with, and the review of internal materials from, industry associations and chambers of commerce. Considering the highly developed private economy in the Yangtze River Delta region and the active nature of these groups, this study selected industry associations and chambers of commerce in Hangzhou, Ningbo, Wenzhou, Wuxi, Shanghai, and other places.

1.1 Questionnaire Design and Distribution

Questionnaire design is inseparable from pre-survey assessment. Scholars have discussed how to ensure the rationality of questionnaire design through panel discussions, in-depth individual interviews, and pre-surveys (Fowler 2010). Before the survey's questionnaire was issued, a group of experts from the Research Center for Social Organizations and Social Governance of Zhejiang University was convened many times to discuss the questionnaire. The heads of the relevant industry associations and chambers of commerce were then invited for in-depth interviews

Y. Shen, *The Policy Participation of Business Associations in China*,
https://doi.org/10.1007/978-981-96-1096-9_4

regarding the questionnaire's content, wording, and concept, which led to many modifications. After the first version of the questionnaire was drafted, a small-scale pre-survey evaluation was carried out in Hangzhou to investigate the expected effect and to probe for any remaining defects in the questionnaire. Finally, the survey questionnaire was divided into three sections (see Appendix 1 for details).

The first section of the questionnaire collects the basic information of the responding industry association or chamber of commerce. This includes when it was established, who founded it, staff size, authority to conduct business, annual income, source of funds, financial management, membership ratio of small- and medium-sized companies, etc.

The second section focuses on the target audiences for the policy participation of the industry associations and chambers of commerce and the manner of participation. For the target audiences of such policy participation, the respondents were asked to state their objectives for policy participation for the preceding three years, including their frequency of policy participation in matters related to the central and local governments, People's Congresses at any level, the Chinese People's Political Consultative Conference, the Party Committees at any level, and the Federation of Industry and Commerce. The policy participation channels used by the industry associations and chambers of commerce are divided into three categories in the questionnaire: information impact, public relations, and trust building.[1] Specifically, it includes "providing policies or suggestions to the government in the form of publications or internal materials", "inviting officials to interpret new policies", "participating in public hearings convened by the government", "supporting academic research related to industry", "providing industrial policy information to the government orally", "submitting information to the media to hold press conferences", "participating in charitable public welfare undertakings", "through banquets, exchanging policy information with officials", etc.

The third section is meant to capture the attitudes and perceptions concerning the participation of the industry associations and chambers of commerce policy. Respondents were asked to assess the impact of policy

[1] This classification is detailed in the paper by Deng and Kennedy (2010). This classification originally appeared in a paper by Hillman and Hitt (1999), and Deng and Kennedy have made a comparison of the classification in Hillman & Hitt's paper with some improvements.

engagement in their industry associations, attitudes that should play a role in a given situation, and what actions would be taken to achieve the purpose of policy participation.

From June to August 2012, the research team of the Research Center for Social Organizations and Social Governance of Zhejiang University distributed questionnaires at the annual meeting of provincial industry associations and chambers of commerce held by the Zhejiang Provincial Department of Civil Affairs and the annual meeting of Ningbo Industry Associations and Chambers of Commerce held by the Ningbo Civil Affairs Bureau. The distribution of questionnaires to the Wenzhou Industry Associations and Wuxi Industry Associations and Chamber of Commerce was facilitated by the local Federation of Industry and Commerce in both places.[2] The questionnaires were completed by the president, secretary-general, or chairman of the industry association or chamber of commerce.

In 2012, a total of 178 industry associations and chambers of commerce attended the annual conference of Zhejiang Province-wide Industry Associations and Chambers of Commerce, and a total of 68, the annual meeting of Ningbo Industry Associations and Chambers of Commerce. Thus, 178 questionnaires and 68 questionnaires were distributed at each event, respectively. With the help of the local Federation of Industry and Commerce, 145 questionnaires were distributed in Wenzhou City, and 124, in Wuxi City. Among the 125 valid questionnaires collected, 34 were from Zhejiang Province Provincial Industry Associations and Chambers of Commerce, 35 from Ningbo Industry Associations and Chambers of Commerce, 19 from the Wenzhou Industry Associations and Chambers of Commerce, and

[2] According to the requirements of the Regulations on the Management of Social Groups, local industry associations and chambers of commerce need the local civil affairs department (bureau) to be responsible for registration management and annual inspection. Considering the cost and scale of research, it is ideal to choose the annual meeting of industry associations and chambers of commerce to distribute questionnaires. As of September 2012, when the first phase of the research done by the Research Center for Social Organization and Social Governance of Zhejiang University was completed, most of the industry associations and chambers of commerce in Wenzhou and Wuxi had the Wenzhou Federation of Industry and Commerce and the Wuxi Federation of Industry and Commerce as their business supervisory units. It was therefore more conducive to grasping the current situation of policy participation of industry associations and chambers of commerce through the Wenzhou and Wuxi Municipal Federation of Industry and Commerce.

37 from Wuxi Industry Associations and Chambers of Commerce. The effective recovery rate of the questionnaire was 19.1%, 51.5%, 31.1%, and 29.8%, respectively. Later, taking the proportional requirements of the different professional supervisory units of the chambers of commerce and industry associations into account, there was a supplementary distribution of survey questionnaires in the form of interviews. In Zhejiang province, 8 of these questionnaires were distributed to provincial industry associations. Therefore, a total of 133 valid questionnaires were recovered.

According to the information released by the Zhejiang Provincial Civil Affairs Department, the Ningbo Civil Affairs Bureau, the Wenzhou Civil Affairs Bureau, and the Wuxi Civil Affairs Bureau, at the end of 2011, there were in total 258 industry associations and chambers of commerce in Zhejiang Province, 110 in Ningbo, 145 in Wenzhou, and 124 in Wuxi. The overall effective recovery rate for questionnaires was 25.4%, Wenzhou City had the lowest effective recovery rate of 13.1%; Ningbo City had the highest effective recovery rate of 51.5%.

Table 1 describes the relevant data for samples and populations. In the Zhejiang Industry Associations and Chambers of Commerce sample, the proportions of different professional supervisory units were 50%, while the proportions of different professional supervisory units overall were 45.7% and 54.3%, the difference between the sample and the population structure ratio is 4.3%. The proportion of different business units in the sample structure of the Ningbo City Chamber of Commerce was 47.3% and 52.7%, respectively, while the proportion of different business units in the overall sample structure was 57.1% and 42.9%, respectively, with a difference of 9.9%. The proportion of different business units in the sample structure of the Wuxi City Chamber of Commerce was 97.3% and 2.7%, respectively, while the proportion of different business units in the sample structure of the Wuxi City Chamber of Commerce was 97.6% and 2.4%, respectively, with a structural difference of 0.3%. Collectively, the sample structure being basically consistent with the overall structure, the sample is well representative of the total.

Table 1 Comparison of sample structure and overall structure

		Number of samples (structure ratio)	*The number of the population (structure ratio)*	*Number of samples/ population*
Zhejiang Province	EIC & FIC	21 (50.0%)	11B (45.7%)	17.8%
	Subtotals for	21 (50.0%)	140 (54.3%)	1.0%
	specific business authorities	42 (100%)	258 (100%)	2.3%
Ningbo City	EIC & FIC	20 (57.1%)	52b (47.3%)	38.5%
	Subtotals for	15 (42.9%)	58 (52.7%)	25.9%
	specific business authorities	35 (100%)	110 (100%)	31.8%
Wenzhou City	EIC & FIC	16 (84.2%)	122c (84.1%)	13.1%
	Subtotals for	3 (15.8%)	23 (15.9%)	13.0%
	specific business authorities	19 (100%)	145 (100%)	13.1%
Wuxi City	EIC & FIC	36 (97.3%)	121(97.6%)	29.8%
	Subtotals for	1(2.7%)	3 (2.4%)	33.3%
	specific business authorities	37 (100%)	124 (100%)	29.8%
Total		133	637	20.9%

Note EIC is the abbreviation of Economy and Information Committee; FIC is the Federation of Industry and Commerce. The competent departments for specific business refer to the competent units of specific industry associations and chambers of commerce such as construction departments (bureaus), water conservancy departments (bureaus), and quality supervision bureaus. a. The business department of 115 industry associations and chambers of commerce is the Economic Information Commission, and the business department of 3 industry associations and chambers of commerce is the Federation of Industry and Commerce; b. The business departments of 44 industry associations and chambers of commerce are the Economic Information Commission, and the business departments of 8 industry associations and chambers of commerce are the Federation of Industry and Commerce; c. There is no one industry association and chamber of commerce whose business authority is the Economic Information Commission, and Wenzhou and Wuxi City made the Federation of Industry and Commerce the business department of industry associations and chambers of commerce in 2006 and 2007, respectively

1.2 Case Interviews

From September 2013 to May 2014, four industry associations and chambers of commerce were interviewed. They were selected based on their survey responses, basic characteristics, external environments, ability to support policy participation, government policy objectives, and their history in policy participation events. The structured interviews lasted from 60 to 90 min and sought to answer the following questions: First, in what events do the industry associations and chambers of commerce participate in policy formulation? Second, what efforts have they made in policy participation? Third, how did the relevant government departments act and respond? Fourth, what are the results of their policy participation? The case interviews were conducted by the author with the head of the industry associations and chamber of commerce, the secretary-general, chairman, or president of the associations, as well as officials of relevant government departments (see Appendix 2 for a detailed outline of the interviews).

The four industry associations and chambers of commerce interviewed in this study and the reason for choosing them are as follows: (1) Taishun Small Hydropower Industry Association because it sought the fair formulation and implementation of small hydropower price policies; (2) Wenzhou E-commerce Industry Association because it advocates for and formulates and implements Wenzhou's e-commerce development policies; (3) Shanghai Indoor Environment Purification Industry Association because it advocates for and implements the policy of "Shanghai Air Purification Engineering Professional Contracting Enterprise Qualification Certification"; and (4) Zhejiang Bicycle and Electric Vehicle Industry Association because its efforts have affected the policy content of the national, provincial, municipal, and other administrative levels regarding the management of electric bicycles.

2 Variable Definition and Measurement

2.1 *Industry Associations and Chambers of Commerce: Policy Participation Capacity*

As the literature shows, the policy participation ability of industry associations and chambers of commerce includes not only the initiatives of their independent organizational structures, but also the initiatives of their internal and external resource mobilization and independent action, which is specifically manifested in the representativeness, autonomy, human resources, and the financial resources of the entity. Correspondingly, the policy participation ability of the association or chamber can be divided into four dimensions: "generation path", "business supervisory unit", "personnel independence", and "financial independence". In terms of specific measurement indicators, the "generation method" of the industry association or chambers of commerce was divided into "government formation" and "enterprise or businessman formation". The "professional supervisory unit" was divided into "Economic and Information Commission", "Local Federation of Industry and Commerce", and "Specific Business Authority" (such as the Construction Department or Bureau and other management of specific industry associations and chambers of commerce). Due to the large number of industry associations and chambers of commerce under the Economic and Information Commission and the local Federation of Industry and Commerce, their policy interests will be relatively scattered. The specific business authorities are often affiliated with a small number of specific industry associations and chambers of commerce and have close policy interests. Thus, the Economic and Information Commission and the local Federation of Industry and Commerce are grouped together. Specific business supervisory units are grouped into another category. "Number of retired officials" and "autonomy in the hiring of the Secretary-General" were used as indicators of "independence of personnel". "The proportion of government financial support for industry associations and chambers of commerce in the total income of chambers of commerce" and "whether the financial management of industry associations and chambers of commerce is autonomous" were used as indicators to measure "financial independence" (see Table 2).

2.2 Government Policy Willingness and Its Measurement

Consonant with the existing literature, the government's policy will is defined in this study as the attitude and motivation expressed by the government in the policy process, which is specifically manifested in the active transmission of policy information, the granting of policy priority paths, and the active empowerment of policy implementation power (Yu et al. 2014). In terms of specific measurement indicators, considering the difficulty of quantifying the government's policy will and the availability of data, the questionnaire uses "whether you are acting as a decision-making consultant or committee member at all levels to make suggestions" as the indicator to measure the government's policy will. Answers were either "yes" or "no".

Table 2 Measurement dimensions and indicators of policy participation capacity of industry associations and chambers of commerce

	Measurement dimensions	*Measurement metrics*
Industry consultations Policy engagement	1. Generation method	(1) Government formation (2) Formation of enterprises or businessmen
	2. Business supervisory unit	(1) Economic and Information Commission; Federation of Commerce and Industry (2) Specific business authorities
	3 Personnel Independence	(1) The number of retired officials (2) Whether the secretary-general is autonomous in hiring
	4. Financial independence	(1) The proportion of the government's financial support for industry associations and chambers of commerce and industry associations to the total income of chambers of commerce (2) Whether the financial management of industry associations and chambers of commerce is autonomous

2.3 *Policy Participation of Industry Associations and Chambers of Commerce and Their Measurement*

The policy participation of industry associations and chambers of commerce was divided into three different types: "policy advocacy", "participation in decision-making", and "private benefit government". Drawing on Deng and Kennedy (2010)'s research on policy lobbying of industry associations and chambers of commerce, the enthusiasm of the policy lobbying by the industry association or chamber of commerce was measured by its "frequency of policy participation of industry associations and chambers of commerce in the past three years" on the Likert-5 scale. "Never": "1"; "At least once a year": "2"; "At least once every six months": "3"; "At least once a month": "4"; and "at least once a week ": "5".

2.4 *Other Control Variables*

Studies have found that other factors also affect the policy participation of industry associations and chambers of commerce. (1) "How long industry associations and chambers of commerce have been established"—In general, the shorter the establishment of an industry association or chamber of commerce, the more active it is in policy participation (Kennedy and Deng 2012). (2) "SME membership ratio"—The higher the percentage of SME members, the more likely it is to engage in policy engagement activities on behalf of the interests of its members (Kennedy 2005, 2009). (3) "Industry association and chamber of commerce size"—This includes the number of employees and members, which may also affect the association or chamber's ability to mobilize resources for policy participation. (4) "Annual income"—For the industry association or chamber of commerce, the higher the income, the more likely it will mobilize its investment funds to carry out policy participation activities. (5) "Administrative level"—In terms of resource coverage and mobilization capacity for policy participation, provincial industry associations and chambers of commerce are equipped with more resources than those at the prefecture and city level, and are more likely to participate in policy engagement.

In summary, the independent variables (IV) of the policy participation of industry associations and chambers of commerce are the policy participation ability and government policy will of industry associations and chambers of commerce. The dependent variable (DV) is the frequency of policy participation of industry associations and chambers of commerce over the past three years. The control variables (CV) are the date the industry association or chamber of commerce was established and the proportion and size of its SME members, its annual income, and its administrative level (see Table 3).

Table 3 Definitions of variables and their measurement of industry associations and chambers of commerce policy participation

	Variable definitions	*Variable interpretation*	*Variable measurement*
Dependent variable (DV)	The degree of policy involvement of industry associations and chambers of commerce	In the past three years, industry associations and chambers of commerce have carried out policy participation frequency	"Never": 1; "At least once a year": 2; "at least once every six months": 3; "At least once a month": 4; "At least once a week", 5
Argument (IV)	Ability to participate in the policies of industry associations and chambers of commerce	1. Generation method 2. Business authorities 3. Personnel Independence 4. Financial independence	1. "Founded by a business or businessman": 1, "Government Transformation or Government Creation" 2. "Specific government departments" 1, "Economic and Information Commission or Federation of Industry and Commerce" 10; 3. The number of retired officials is a specific value; Autonomy of the Secretary-General: Yes: 1; No: 0; 4. The proportion of government financial support is a specific value; Financial management autonomy: Yes, 1; No, 0

(continued)

Table 3 (continued)

	Variable definitions	*Variable interpretation*	*Variable measurement*
	Government policy will	Whether the government has given industry associations and chambers of commerce priority channels for policy participation, such as being a government decision-making consultant or member of an advisory committee, and having priority channels for policy transmission	"Yes": 1; "No": 0
Control variables (CV)	Industry associations and chambers of commerce	Number of employees Number of members	Specific values Specific values
	Annual income	The value of annual revenue for the year	Specific values
	Percentage of SME membership	SME Member/Total Member	Specific percentage
	Date of establishment	Years of establishment	Specific values
	The administrative level at which it is located	Provincial, municipal	Comparison with provincial industry associations and chambers of commerce

Appendix 1: Survey Questionnaires

Questionnaires on Development of Industry Associations and Chambers of Commerce (IACC)

Dear IACC leader,

To better understand the development of IACCs in China, especially the participation of IACCs in public policy formulation and implementation, we invite you to participate in this survey. Your answers will affect the development of China's industrial organizations.

For the multiple-choice questions, please check the option you think is appropriate. For the fill-in-the blank questions, please answer according to your experience.

Thank you so much for your support and cooperation!

Zhejiang University Research Center for Social Organizations and Social Governance

July 2012

Your position in your association: ______________________.

I. Basic conditions

1. Name of your association ______, Founding date ______, Supervisory agency _______, Number of institutional members ________ __, Number of individual members __________, The proportion of institutional members in total local companies in the industry ______ _%

2. Numbers of employees in your association ______, number of full-time employees ______, number of full-time employees with an associate degree or above ________, number of employees with government work experience _______.

3. Organizational revenue of year 2011 ______ (RMB 10 thousand) and spending of year 2011 ________ (RMB 10 thousand) of year 2011, Collection rate of membership fees of year 2011 _______ %

4. Revenue Composition of year 2011.

Source	Proportion of total revenue	Spending category	Proportion of total spending
Membership fees		Daily operation (including wages, administration fees, and travel expenses)	
Donations		Member services (training, consulting, exhibitions, and publications)	
Government funding (including appropriations, subsidies, and awards)		Contributions to the society (donations, student aid)	
Service charges from members		Other	
Service charges through government Purchases			
Sales (including publications)			
Investment (e.g., interest, dividends, bonuses)			
Other (e.g., fines paid by members)			

5. The direct reason for establishing your association:
A. transformation of government agency B. established by government C. Self-establishment.

6. Does your association have the authority to do any of the following (check all that apply):
A. Elect the president B. Select the secretary C. Hire full-time employees D. Manage finances independently E. Develop organizational plans F. Participate in charity G. Organize business activities.

7. Which category does your association belong to (check all that apply):
A. Traditional industry B. Strategic emerging industry C. Local pillar industry.

8. The level of importance the local government attaches to your association is
A. High B. relatively high C. Average D. Relatively low E. Low.

10. Your association hosts the general assembly every ___ year, the number of board members is _____, the board has ____ meeting(s) a year. The attendance rate of the last board meeting was _____%. Is there a formal division of labor within the council?
A. Yes B. No.

II. Policy Advocacy

1. In the past year, has your association used the following methods to make policy suggestions to the government?

Make proposals to congressional representatives or Chinese People' s Political Consultative Conference (CPPCC) through the association' s members	A. Yes B. No
Make proposals as a consultant or committee member at all levels of government	A. Yes B. No
Formally or informally write to government agencies or higher-level industrial associations, to have an impact	A. Yes B. No
Make proposals through the All-China Federation of Industry and Commerce (ACFIC)	A. Yes B. No

2. On average, over the past three years, how often has your association made policy suggestions to the following authorities? (Check the appropriate box).

Frequency / Object to propose	At least once a week	At least once a month	At least once every half year	At least once a year	Never
The central government					
The National People's congress					
The National Committee CPPCC					
The Central Committee of CPC					
The National ACFIC					
Local government					
Local People's Congress					
Local Committee of the CPPCC					
Local Committee of CPC					
Local FIC					

3. On average, over the past three years, how often has your association used the following methods to make policy recommendations (Check in the appropriate box).

Methods \ Frequency	At least once a week	At least once a month	At least once every half year	At least once a year	Never
Publications or internal bulletins					
Policies or suggestions					
Invite officials to explain new policies					
Attend public hearings hosted by the government					
Support academic research related to industrial policy					
Orally provide industrial policy related information to the government					
Provide information to the media					
Host press conferences					
Participate in charity events					
Communicate with public officials on policy information through banquets					

4. Please select how much you agree with the following statements by checking the appropriate box (5-4-3-2-1).

	Completely agree	Somewhat agree	Neutral	Somewhat disagree	Completely disagree
It is very important for industrial associations and chambers of commerce (IACC) to establish a good relationship with the government.					
A good relationship with the government official is the key for IACC to influence government policies.					
Your association maintains a good relationship with government officials.					
Large member enterprises are more influential on the government than small member enterprises .					
The influence of your association on the government has greatly improved over the past three years.					
Your association is more influential than most associations.					
Your association is more influential than large associations.					
Your association has smooth channels to safeguard the interest of the industry.					
Through your association' s efforts, government policies are more in line with the interests of the industry.					
The policy suggestions proposed by board members are more likely to be conveyed to the government than the ones proposed by non-board members.					

5. Has your association successfully influenced policy-making at the central or local government level?
A. Yes. B. No.

6. Has your association influenced changes in or the abolishment of a policy at the central or local government level?
A. Yes. B. No

7. If the government and most members of your association disagree on a policy, then what will your association do?
A. Maintain the position of the majority of the members and try to persuade the government to accept the view of your members.
B. Accept the government's position and try to persuade the majority of your members to accept it too.
C. Find a comprise between A. and B.

8. When there is a conflict between the interests of the leading company in your industry interest and the overall interest of the industry, your association will:
A. Completely focus on the overall interest of the industry.
B. Completely focus on the interest of the members.
C. Find a comprise between A. and B.

9. If the government is about to formulate a policy affecting your industry, then which action does your association usually take?
A. Wait for the policy to be promulgated and consider a strategy to influence the policy if problems are discovered.
B. Try to influence the policy and its promulgation during the process of policy formation.

Appendix 2: Interview Questionnaires Outlines

Interview Questionnaires on the Policy Participation of Industrial Association and Chambers of Commerce.

Dear IACC leader,

To better understand the development of IACC in China, especially on the participation of IACC in public policy formulation and implementation, we invite you to take 60–90 min out of your busy schedule to complete this interview. We promise to keep the information provided in this interview confidential and use it for academic research only.

Thank you so much for your support and cooperation!

Zhejiang University Research Center for Social Organizations and Social Governance

March 2014

I. Basic situation

Please briefly introduce the history and status of your association. Please include: date of establishment, reason for establishment (main body), supervisory agency, number of members, percentage of members in the industry, number of employees (both full-time and part-time), number of people with government work experience, annual revenue, annual spending, categories of annual revenue and their percentages, and milestones in history.

II. Participation of IACC in policy formulation and implementation

1 Has your association ever carried out policy advocacy or influenced the formulation, modification, and implementation of policies?

2 If yes, what were the policy activities? What specific efforts has your association made in carrying out policy activities? For example: Which government agencies have you communicated with, and how have you communicated with the government and member companies?

3 What difficulties did your association encounter in carrying out those policy activities? What measures have you used to solve such problems?

4 In carrying out those policy activities, how did the government and its relevant agencies respond to your association's policy advocacy? Support or strongly oppose?

5 Finally, have the policy activities of your association achieved satisfactory results? For example: the successful formulation or modification of a policy?

References

Deng G and Kennedy S. Big business and industry association lobbying in China: The paradox of contrasting styles. The China Journal, 2010, 63: 101-125.

Fowler F. J. Improving Survey Questions: Design and Evaluation. Chongqing: Chongqing University Press, 2010.

Hillman A J, and Hitt M A. Corporate political strategy formulation: A model of approach, participation, and strategy decisions. The Academy of Management Review, 1999, 24(4): 825-842.

Kennedy S. Comparing formal and informal lobbying practices in China: The capital's ambivalent embrace of capitalists. China Information, 2009, 23(2): 195-222.

Kennedy S. The Business of Lobbying in China. Cambridge: Harvard University Press, 2005.

Yu J, Shen Y, and Zhou J. From dual management to compliance regulation--The reconstruction of the regulatory System of industry associations and chambers of commerce in the era of comprehensive deepening reform. Journal of Zhejiang University (Humanities and Social Sciences), 2014, 44(4): 107-116.

CHAPTER 5

Introduction to the Factors Influencing the Policy Participation of Chinese Industry Associations and Chambers of Commerce: Analysis of Large-Sample Data

This chapter examines the relationship between the state and society in China by analyzing industry association and chamber of commerce policy participation data. First, the study examined a large sample of descriptive statistics of the target objects, participation methods and channels, attitudes and perceptions, and policy participation results of selected industry associations and chambers of commerce. Second, a large-sample regression analysis tested this study's first two hypotheses.

Hypothesis 1 The more robust the policy participation ability of an industry association or chamber of commerce, the more it will participate in the policy process.

Hypothesis 2 The greater the priority path for policy the government gives to an industry association or chamber of commerce, the more it will participate in the policy process.

1 Policy Participation of Industry Associations and Chambers of Commerce

Policy participation of industry associations and chambers of commerce includes their target objectives, methods and channels of participation, attitudes and views, attitudes toward the conflicts of interests among

Y. Shen, *The Policy Participation of Business Associations in China*,
https://doi.org/10.1007/978-981-96-1096-9_5

group members, and the results of their policy endeavors. Empirical evidence shows these groups have diverse target objects, channels, and participation methods. Nearly one-third have successfully influenced policy formulation or revision or even stopped a policy from being implemented through their interactions with the government.

Table 1 describes the target audiences for the policy participation efforts of industry associations and chambers of commerce. The data shows they directed most of their energy toward local institutions. Only 30.1% of these groups targeted the central government; 88.3% targeted local governments. The NPC, CPPCC, Party Committee, and Federation of Industry and Commerce (AIC) among the policy participation targets of industry associations and chambers of commerce also point more to the local level, which shows that the policy participation of local industry associations and chambers of commerce surveyed has more influence on local policies. Statistics have also shown that local governments are the most involved and frequent targets of industry associations and chambers of commerce in all local-level institutions. 43.6% of industry associations and chambers of commerce participated in policy events at least once a year. 27.7% participated in policy events once every six months. The local federation of industry and commerce is the least involved body among the sample cohort, with only 21.8% of its members participating in policy events at least once a year. The policy participation targets of industry associations and chambers of commerce were diverse, but local groups focused more on local institutions, especially local governments. This fact shows that the policy participation of local industry associations and chambers of commerce occurs more at the local level.

Table 2 describes the policy participation methods used by industry associations, divided into information influence, public relations, and trust building. Among them, "information impact" is the most commonly used way and method for industry associations and chambers of commerce to participate in policies. 77.6% of industry associations and chambers of commerce impact policy information "in the form of publications or internal materials" at least once a year. 55.1% of industry associations and chambers of commerce "provide policy information orally" at least once a year. 38.3% of industry associations and chambers of commerce hold a policy meeting once a year. "Public relations" is another essential way for industry associations and chambers of commerce to participate in policies. 60.7% of industry associations and chambers make full use of the media

Table 1 The target audience for the policy participation of industry associations and chambers of commerce

	Never (%)	*Annually (%)*	*Semi-Annually (%)*	*Monthly (%)*	*Weekly (%)*	*Samples (N)*
Central Government	69.9	14.0	8.6	6.5	1.0	93
National People's Congress	87.1	3.2	6.5	2.2	1.1	93
National Committee of the CPPCC	88.2	3.2	4.3	3.2	1.1	93
Party Central Organization	86.0	3.2	5.4	5.4	0	93
All-China Federation of Industry and Commerce	100.0	0	0	0	0	55
Local Government	11.7	43.6	27.7	16.0	1.0	94
Local People's Congress	62.8	24.5	6.4	6.4	0	94
Local Committee of the CPPCC	62.8	23.4	7.4	8.4	0	94
Local Party Committee	70.2	12.8	6.4	10.6	0	94
Local Federation of Industry and Commerce	78.2	14.5	5.5	1.8	0	55

to promote their policy information at least once a year. In "trust building", communicating with officials through banquets is the leading means of policy exchange in industry associations and chambers of commerce. 43.0% of industry associations and chambers of commerce have banquets with officials at least once a year. 29.9% of industry associations and chambers of commerce achieve policy exchanges with officials once a year through banquets, and 11.2% of trade associations and chambers of commerce do so every six months, with these banquets usually being held during the mid-year or year-end events. The methods of policy participation employed by industry associations and chambers of commerce were diverse, and formal participation was more than informal participation.

Table 3 describes the attitudes and perceptions of industry associations on policy participation, including views on the importance and effect of

Table 2 Methods of policy participation by industry associations and chambers of commerce

		Never (%)	*Annually (%)*	*Semi-Annually (%)*	*Monthly (%)*	*Weekly (%)*	*Samples (N)*
Information	Letters and publications	22.4	21.5	30.8	24.3	1.0	107
Influence	Convene policy meeting	42.1	38.3	18.7	0.9	0	107
	Attend public hearings	69.2	16.8	13.1	0.9	0	107
	Support industry/ government/ academic research	35.5	33.6	24.3	5.6	0.9	107
	Provide information to the government orally	44.9	21.5	18.7	11.2	3.7	107
Public relationship	Provide government information to the media	39.3	22.4	27.1	10.3	0.9	107
	Hold a press conference	74.8	15.0	8.4	1.9	0	107
	Influencing policy through philanthropy	53.3	28.0	15.9	2.8	0	107
Trust building	Exchange policy with officials through banquets	57.0	29.9	11.2	1.9	0	107

relationships in policy participation, the significance of policy influence on associations and chambers of commerce, and the smoothness of policy participation channels. The data shows that 91.7% of industry associations and chambers believe that building good relationships with the government is very important for policy participation, and as many as 76.5% believe that relationships are the key to achieving policy participation of the sample industry associations and chambers of commerce. 61% of the sample respondents admit to having good relationships with government officials, which verifies the importance of social capital in policy participation of industry associations and chambers of commerce. Most industry associations and chambers of commerce affirmed and boasted about their policy participation. 72.7% believed that their policy influence dramatically improved in the past three years; 67.8% believed that industry associations and chambers of commerce had more policy influence than most enterprises; 54.3% agreed that industry associations and chambers of commerce were more influential than large enterprises; 64.3% believed they had effective channels for policy participation; 65.8% believed their policy participation efforts made policies more in line with the interests of the industry. As may be expected, there is a gap between their subjective evaluations of their policy influence and the objective results of such efforts. The former is obviously more optimistic.

Table 4 describes the attitudes and practices of industry associations and chambers of commerce when faced with conflicts of interest among members during policy participation. When the government and most member enterprises had different opinions on a specific policy, 56% of industry associations and chambers of commerce maintained neutral coordination, and 33% believed that they should represent the interests of member enterprises to persuade the government. Only 11% helped the government persuade member enterprises. When the interests of leading enterprises conflicted with the interests of the industry as a whole, 60.9% of industry associations and chambers of commerce chose to defend the interests of the industry; 31.8% of industry associations and chambers of commerce remained neutral and coordinated their interests; only 7.3% decided to safeguard the policy interests of the leading enterprises. Most industry associations and chambers of commerce remained focused on protecting the industry's interests in their policy participation. Still, when there was a policy conflict between the government and members' interests, the attitudes of the industry associations and chambers of commerce were unclear.

Table 3 Attitudes and views of industry associations and chambers of commerce on policy participation

	Totally Agree (%)	*Somewhat Agree (%)*	*Neutral (%)*	*Somewhat Disagree (%)*	*Totally Disagree (%)*	*Sample (N)*
It is very Important to have a good relationship with the Government	64.2	27.5	7.5	0.8	0	120
Relationships are key to policy impact	33.3	43.2	16.2	5.4	1.8	111
Your association has a good relationship with government officials	22.1	38.9	35.4	1.8	1.8	113
Large member companies are more influential than small member companies	37.4	48.7	13.0	0.9	0	115
In the past three years, your policy influence has been greatly improved	18.2	44.5	33.6	2.7	0.9	110
Your association has more influence than most companies	23.2	44.6	26.8	5.4	0	112
Your association is more influential than big corporations	14.3	40.0	37.1	8.6	0	70
Your association has effective policy participation channels	18.6	45.7	32.9	2.9	0	70
Through your association's policy participation efforts, the policy became more in line with the interests of the industry	12.9	52.9	32.9	1.4	0	70

Table 5 describes the practical effect of the policy participation of industry associations and chambers of commerce. 31.9% of industry associations and chambers of commerce reported to have successfully influenced the policy-making process and 27.9% reported to have led to a beneficial policy change, whether through promulgation or cessation. One-third of the industry associations and chambers of commerce succeeded in policy participation in practice. Generally, it is more difficult

Table 4 Attitudes and practices of industry associations and chambers of commerce when faced with conflicts of interest of different subjects in their policy participation

The government disagrees with most member companies on a certain policy	Persuade the Government (%)	Neutral (%)	Persuade Members	Samples (N)
	33.0	56.0	11.0	109
When there is a policy conflict between the interests of leading enterprises and the overall interests of the industry	Industry Interests (%)	Neutral (%)	Leading Enterprises (%)	Samples (N)
	60.9	31.8	7.3	110

Table 5 Industry associations and chambers of commerce policy participation results

Policy engagement results	*Yes (%)*	*No (%)*	*Number of samples (N)*
Success at influencing policymaking	31.9	68.1	119
Success at influencing a policy change or stopping policy enforcement	27.9	72.1	111

for industry associations to influence policy modification or to stop policy implementation than to influence policy formulation.

2 Factors Influencing the Policy Participation of Industry Associations and Chambers of Commerce

Based on the definitions and measurements of the dependent and control variables of policy engagement of trade associations and chambers of commerce in Table 4.3, the following descriptive statistics of each variable and its correlation analysis are presented, which is followed by regression analysis to test the research hypotheses and explore the different influencing factors of policy engagement of trade associations and chambers of commerce.

2.1 *Descriptive Statistics and Correlation Analysis*

Table 5.6 reports the descriptive statistical results for independent, dependent, and control variables. The mean and standard deviation of the generation mode of industry associations and chambers of commerce were 0.754 and 0.432, respectively, indicating that the number of trade associations and chambers of commerce established by enterprises or businesspeople was slightly higher than the number of industry associations and chambers of commerce established by the government. The mean and standard deviation of industry associations and chambers of commerce as government decision-making consultants/advisory committee members or with policy priority transmission channels are 0.300 and 0.462, respectively, indicating that the overall proportion of sample industry associations and chambers of commerce becoming members of government policy advisers or advisory committees is low. The mean and standard deviation of the number of retired officials are 1.197 and 1.149, respectively, indicating that the number of retired officials in the sample varied greatly between different industry associations and chambers of commerce. The mean and standard deviation of the employment autonomy of the secretary-general of industry associations and chambers of commerce are 0.829 and 0.379, respectively, indicating that there was a rather high proportion of sample industry associations and chambers of commerce that allowed for their secretary-general's employment autonomy. The mean and standard deviation of financial management autonomy are 0.737 and 0.443, respectively, indicating that the majority of samples had financial management autonomy. The average and standard deviation of government funding as a proportion of these groups' total annual incomes were 14.008 and 25.603, respectively. This indicates that the proportion of sample industry associations and chambers of commerce receiving government financial support was generally not high, and there were significant differences between different industry associations and chambers of commerce. The average and standard deviation of policy participation frequency of industry associations and chambers of commerce targeting local governments were 2.586 and 0.990, respectively. In other words, the frequency of policy participation of most industry associations and chambers of commerce was between at least once every six months and at least once a year. The descriptive statistical results for the remaining variables are detailed in Table 6.

Table 6 Descriptive statistics of independent, dependent, and control variables

Variable	*Metrics*	*Sample (N)*	*Mean*	*Standard Deviation*	*Minimum Value*	*Maximum Value*
Generation method	Established by business or merchant[a]	122	0.754	0.432	0	1
Human resources	Secretary-General Hiring Autonomy[a]	76	0.829	0.379	0	1
	Number of retired officials	117	1.197	1.149	0	10
Business department	Specific government department[a]	132	0.318	0.468	0	1
Financial resources	Financial management autonomy	76	0.737	0.443	0	1
	Ratio of government subsidy to total income (%)	95	14.008	25.603	0	100
Government gives priority to policy channels	As a government decision-making consultant/ member of the advisory committee or with a policy priority delivery channel[a]	70	0.300	0.462	0	1
Dependent variable	The frequency of policy participation of the target government	99	2.586	0.990	1	5
Control variable	Number of employees	129	4.667	2.575	1	14
	Number of member companies (logged)	129	4.920	0.880	0.693	8.189
	Annual Income (10,000 yuan, logged)	97	3.406	1.071	0.815	6.319

(continued)

Table 6 (continued)

Variable	*Metrics*	*Sample (N)*	*Mean*	*Standard Deviation*	*Minimum Value*	*Maximum Value*
	SME[b]	91	69.890	25.033	0	100
	Established	125	2000	7.693	1980	2012
	Administrative Area (Zhejiang = 1; Ningbo = 2; Wenzhou = 3; Wuxi = 4	133	–	–	1	4

[a]Dummy variable
[b]Small and medium-sized enterprises

Table 7 presents the correlation between the indicators of the independent variables. At the 95% confidence interval, the method of formation of the industry association or chamber of commerce is positively correlated with the number of retired officials serving in it, negatively correlated with the hiring autonomy of the secretary-general, negatively correlated with specific government departments, positively correlated with the hiring autonomy of the industry associations and chambers of commerce and the autonomy of financial management. However, the absolute value of the above four correlation coefficients is not very high, with the highest value at 0.2840. The above correlation also shows that, to a certain extent, the establishment of industry associations and chambers of commerce by enterprises or businesspeople does not necessarily mean that there was necessarily autonomy in human resources. However, no significant correlation was found between the "government-given policy participation priority path" and other indicators of independent variables.

Table 8 presents the descriptive statistics of dependent variables at different sample collection points. Among them, 6 provincial industry associations and chambers of commerce in Zhejiang Province participated in policy events at least once a month. 10 Wuxi industry associations and chambers of commerce carried out policy participation activities at least monthly. And 6 Ningbo industry associations and chambers of commerce never lobby the government. The largest number of sample respondents reported lobbying the government every six months or once a year: 22 from Zhejiang Province, 22 from the Ningbo Industry Associations, 16 from Wuxi, and 9 from Wenzhou.

Table 7 Correlation analysis between indicators of independent variables

	Established by a business or merchant[a]	*Secretary-General Hiring Autonomy*[a]	*Number of retired officials*	*Specific government department*[a]	*Financial management autonomy*[a]	*Government subsidy as a percentage of total income (%)*
Established by a business or merchant[a]	1					
Secretary-General Hiring Autonomy[a]	**0.2323	1				
Number of retired officials	**– 0.2840	– 0.2573	1			
Specific government department[a]	**– 0.1741	0.0273	0.0041	1		
Financial management autonomy[a]	– 0.0117	**0.2288	– 0.0494	– 0.0176	1	
Government subsidy as a percentage of total income (%)	0.0462	– 0.0724	0.0266	– 0.0195	– 0.2484	1
As a government decision-making consultant/ member of the advisory committee or with a policy priority delivery channel	– 0.0169	– 0.0819	– 0.0056	0.2445	0.0527	0.1330

* < 0.10; ** < 005; *** < 0.01
[a]Dummy variable

2.2 *Regression Analysis*

Since the dependent variable is a categorical variable of the Likert-5 scale, the available data are not well suited for analysis by ordinary least squares. Among all the multinomial logistic regression models for the ordered dependent variable, this research used cumulative or proportional odds

Table 8 Descriptive statistics for dependent variable at different sample collections

	Never	*Annually*	*Biannually*	*Monthly*	*Weekly*	*Subtotal*	*No Response*	*Total*
All of Zhejiang Province	0	9	13	4	2	28	14	42
Ningbo	6	16	6	0	0	28	7	35
Wenhzou	2	7	2	3	0	14	5	19
Wuxi	3	9	7	9	1	29	8	37
Total	11	41	28	16	3	99	34	133

models because robust standard errors can be used to deal with potential heteroscedasticity problems. Multiple imputation is more effective at dealing with missing data than traditional methods such as culling (King, Honaker, Joseph and Scheve, 2001; Schafer, 1999), so this study used multiple substitution to deal with missing values.

Table 9 presents the results of bivariate regression analysis for the dependent variable and each independent variable. There is statistical significance between the three independent variables and the dependent variable (formation method of the industry association or chamber of commerce generation, the number of retired officials, and the priority policy channel given by the government). The results show that the more priority given to the policy channel of an industry association or chamber of commerce by the government, the greater their policy participation will be. The greater the number of retired officials in an industry association or chamber of commerce, the more involved the entity will be in policy, and those industry associations or chambers of commerce that were established by enterprises or businesspeople engaged in policy participation less often.

Table 10 presents the regression analysis results of the influencing factors of policy participation of industry associations and chambers of commerce. Model (1) shows the regression results between different independent variables and the dependent variables. Model (2) shows the regression results as between independent variables, control variables, and dependent variables after adding the control variables from model (1).

The statistics of model (1) and model (2) together show that:

Table 9 Bivariate regression analysis of individual variables vs variables

Variables	*Index*	*(1)*	*(2)*	*(3)*	*(4)*	*(5)*	*(6)*	*(7)*
Method of founding	Established by a business or merchant	*–0.806 (0.436)						
Human resources	Secretary-general hiring autonomy		0.215 (0.523)					
	Number of retired officials			*0.360 (0.211)				
Business depart-ment	Specific government department				–0.450 (0.395)			
Financial resources	Financial management autonomy					0.386 (0.571)		
	Government subsidy as a percentage of total income (%)						–0.007 (0.1010)	
Government gives priority to policy channels	As a government decision-making consultant/advisory committee member							***1.514 (0.474)
Prob. > F		0.0654	0.6810	0.0895	0.2554	0.5001	0.4906	0.0019
N		133	133	133	133	133	133	133
Imputations		30	30	30	30	30	30	30

Robust standard errors are in parentheses
* < 0.10; ** < 005; *** < 0.01

Among generation methods, those industry associations and chambers of commerce established by enterprises or businesspeople had less policy participation than those established by the government. It was weakened after adding the control variable, but its statistical significance was still significant within the 90% confidence interval, which indicates that the method of formation did affect the frequency policy participation by

Table 10 Regression analysis results of factors influencing policy participation of 10 industry associations and chambers of commerce

Variables	*Index*	*(1)*	*(2)*
Method of founding	Established by a business or merchant	**– 1.069 (0.477)	*– 0.993 (0.571)
Human resources	Secretary-General Hiring Autonomy	0.518 (0.632)	0.148 (0.699)
	Number of retired officials	0.256 (0.316)	0.139 (0.405)
Business department	Specific government department	– 0.707 (0.440)	– 0.830 (0.518)
Financial resources	Financial management autonomy	0.349 (0.619)	0.365 (0.675)
	Government subsidy as a percentage of total income (%)	– 0.012 (0.011)	– 0.015 (0.014)
Government gives priority to policy channels	As a government decision-making consultant / advisory committee member	***1.602 (0.490)	***1.814 (0.568)
Control variable	Number of employees		– 0.006 (0.013)
	Number of member companies (logged)		0.491 (0.332)
	Annual Income (10,000 yuan, logged)		0.041 (0.323)
	SME Proportion (%)		0.007 (0.013)
	Established		0.006 (0.033)
	Ningbo [Based in Zhejiang Province]		**– 1.385 (0.555)
	Wenzhou [Based in Zhejiang Province]		– 0.900 (0.910)
	Wuxi [Based in Zhejiang Province]		– 0.306 (0.790)
Prob. > F		0.0094	0.0170
N		133	133

Robust standard errors are in parentheses
* < 0.10; ** < 005; *** < 0.01

industry associations and chambers of commerce. Therefore, Hypothesis 1(a) is not supported.[1]

Regarding autonomy, the indicators of business authorities of measurement industry associations and chambers of commerce and the frequency of policy participation failed to show statistical significance. Therefore, Hypothesis 1(b) is not supported.[2]

In terms of financial resources, the measurement of financial resources indicators of industry associations and chambers of commerce and the frequency of policy participation also failed to show statistical significance. Therefore, 1(c) is not supported.[3]

In terms of human resources, the number of retired officials also showed statistical significance in bivariate regression analysis. Still, after adding other independent variables, it no longer showed statistical significance, indicating that the causal relationship between the two could not be completely determined. However, there was no statistical significance between the Secretary-General's hiring autonomy and the dependent variable. Therefore, 1(d) is not supported.[4]

For policy channels, even if the industry associations and chambers of commerce are given greater priority by the government, the statistical results are still significant within the 99% confidence interval even after adding the control variables. This indicates that the government policy and industry association policy participation both play an extremely important role. Therefore, Hypothesis 2, "The more the industry associations and chambers of commerce have priority paths for policy participation given by the government, the more policy participation of the industry associations and chambers of commerce" is established.

The regression statistical results therefore refute the original hypothesis 1. The regression results verify the original hypothesis 2. In short, government policy plays an extremely important role in the policy participation of industry associations and chambers of commerce. The policy

[1] 1(a) Hypothesis 1(a): The stronger the representativeness of an industry association or chamber of commerce the more policy participation it will undertake.

[2] Hypothesis 1(b): The stronger the autonomy of an industry association or chamber of commerce, the more policy participation it will undertake.

[3] Hypothesis 1(c): The more independent the financial resources of an industry association or chamber of commerce, the more policy participation it will undertake.

[4] Hypothesis 1(d): The more independent the human resources of an industry association or chamber of commerce, the more policy participation it will undertake.

participation capacity of industry associations and chambers of commerce has a relatively weak influence on their policy participation.

2.3 *Summary*

The statistical analysis of data on the policy participation of industry associations and chambers of commerce shows that the government policy will and the policy participation ability of industry associations and chambers of commerce have different effects on the policy participation behavior of industry associations and chambers of commerce. Statistical analysis of the descriptive data reveals the policy participation of contemporary Chinese industry associations and chambers of commerce is focused on many target objects and diverse policy participation channels and methods. Nearly one-third of industry associations and chambers of commerce have successfully influenced the government through policy formulation, policy revision, or policy implementation. Regression analysis shows that the policy participation capacity of industry associations and chambers of commerce has no significant impact on the frequency of policy participation. On the contrary, government policy will have a significant impact on the policy participation of industry associations and chambers of commerce. This is perhaps because after the industry associations and chambers of commerce are supported by the government, their policy participation will become more active, and the frequency of participation will be higher.

Different from existing research conclusions that industry associations and chambers of commerce established by enterprises or businessmen are more active in policy participation than those established by the government (Jiang and He 2012), the statistics of this book show that the industry associations established by enterprises or businessmen have less policy participation than the industry associations established by the government. The possible reason is that government established groups have more official channels for policy participation and more opportunities than those established by enterprises or businessmen. However, the low frequency of policy participation by industry associations and chambers of commerce established by enterprises or businessmen does not mean that their policy participation is not effective. Subsequent research needs to consider the differences in the effectiveness of policy participation in industry associations and chambers of commerce with different generation methods.

However, statistical analysis cannot show neither the continuous and dynamic interaction between the policy capabilities of industry associations and chambers of commerce, nor the mechanisms that enable the strategic interaction between trade associations and government in a changing external environment. The multiple case study analysis presented in the next chapter will explore this area.

References

Jiang H, and He B. A comparative study on the policy participation of trade associations: Nanjing and Wenzhou. Journal of Zhejiang Party School C.P.C., 2012, 1: 27-36.

King G, Honaker J, Joseph A, and Scheve K. Analyzing incomplete political science data: An alternative algorithm for multiple imputation. American Political Science Review, 2001, 95(1): 49-69.

Schafer J L. Multiple imputation: A primer. Statistical Methods in Medical Research, 1999, 8(1): 3-15.

CHAPTER 6

Policy Participation Mechanisms of China's Industry Associations and Chambers of Commerce: A Multi-Case Study

The results of this study's large-sample statistical analysis show that the government's policy objective is the influencing factor for the policy participation of industry associations and chambers of commerce. However, the analysis does not explain the dynamic mechanism of state–society interactions in the process of policy participation of industry associations and chambers of commerce. The government's will is also not static. Industry associations and chambers of commerce exert their own will through their own initiatives. For them, policy participation is a strategic interaction. That process is affected by the strategy deployed by the industry associations and chambers of commerce and the external environment. These important issues need to be demonstrated in the following case studies.

This chapter is structured as follows. First, it presents the basic information of the industry associations and chambers of commerce, their external environments, their ability to engage in policy participation, the government's policy will, the interaction background and process of policy participation events, and the final results of the efforts of industry associations and chambers of commerce to change government behavior. This chapter describes and analyzes the policy participation process of four industry associations and chambers of commerce.

Second, based on the comparative study of these four cases, the continuity and dynamics of the interaction between industry associations and chambers of commerce and the government, as well as the mutual shaping

Y. Shen, *The Policy Participation of Business Associations in China*,
https://doi.org/10.1007/978-981-96-1096-9_6

and regulation of the external environment and strategic interactions, are then discussed.

Finally, the theoretical implications of the results of the multi-case comparative analysis as they relate to state–society relations in China are discussed.

1 The Taishun Small Hydropower Industry Association and Its Effects on the Adjustment and Implementation of the Prices Paid for Small Hydropower on the Grid

Taishun County is in the southern, mountainous area of Wenzhou, where there are many rivers, with more than 110 large and small streams and a total basin area of 1766 km. Its average annual precipitation is 2200 mm. These rich hydraulic resources boast theoretical reserves of 620,000 kilowatts, with an exploitable utilization of 580,000 kilowatts (Wu 2007). Before 1990, most of the hydropower stations in Taishun County were built by the state-owned economy and through collective economic investment. With the development of the private economy and the tension between power supply and demand, in 1993, the Zhejiang provincial government issued its "Notice on Accelerating Hydropower Reform and Promoting Water Conservancy Development". This reform set the on-grid tariff for small hydropower and the investment system for small hydropower, encouraging society to invest in developing small hydropower. With the incentive of small hydropower investment profits and the encouragement of the government's preferential policies, private capital has poured into small hydropower investment and construction.

To better represent and safeguard the interests of small hydropower owners, on December 26, 1996, the country's first small hydropower industry association, the Taishun County Small Hydropower Industry Association (hereafter Taishun Association), came into being. The association membership mainly comprises small hydropower group members and individual members. Membership fees are standardized: each group must pay 1 yuan per kilowatt of capacity per year, and individuals must pay 20 yuan per year. The primary revenue of the association comes from group membership fees and power station sponsorship fees, which account for more than 90%. Regarding the staffing of the association, President Shu Dingmiao was the owner of the hydropower station of the county party committee and served as the president of the county court for two terms. He Xuchang was the executive vice president and had just retired from his post as director of the county's Poverty Alleviation Office, and was familiar with the laws and policies of the hydropower industry. As a mutually beneficial organization voluntarily formed by small hydropower owners, the Taishun Association positions itself as a bridge and link between government departments, power enterprises, and small hydropower owners.

1.1 Policy Participation Paths

To save small hydropower enterprises from losses, increase profits, and strive for fair, just, and reasonable electricity prices, the Taishun Association has carried out effective policy participation in activities such as "requiring the implementation of electricity price policies", "affecting the adjustment of on-grid electricity prices", "petitioning for fair implementation of small hydropower on-grid prices", and "cooperating with other small hydropower industry associations in the province to carry out electricity price policy negotiation games" (Zhu 2007).

1.1.1 1996 to 1997: The association urges the Taishun County Power Supply Bureau to implement the existing electricity price policy

Document No. 59 [1994] of Zhejiang Provincial Price Bureau stipulates that new power stations put into operation after 1994 must uniformly implement the policy of "repaying principal and interest, new electricity, and new prices" in the province. Peak and valley levels were divided; peak power was set at 14 hours, and valley power was set at 10 hours. Document No. 295 [1996] of Zhejiang Provincial Price Bureau stipulates that the electricity price specified in Document No. 59 [1994] is 0.33 yuan/kWh (peak electricity price 0.46 yuan/kWh, valley electricity price 0.115 yuan/kWh) based on 0.44 yuan/kWh (peak electricity price 0.58 yuan/kWh, valley electricity price 0.198 yuan/kWh), which was to be implemented from August 1, 1996. However, the Taishun County Power Supply Bureau failed to implement the new electricity price policy in Document No. 295 [1996] of Zhejiang Provincial Price Bureau. It also arbitrarily reduced the peak electricity to 13.5 hours, which caused enormous losses for the small hydropower owners.

In the spring of 1997, the Taishun Association reported to the Zhejiang Provincial Price Bureau, requesting that relevant local departments and units be urged to strictly implement the document's provisions to maintain the policy's authority. After several report requests, the Zhejiang Provincial Price Bureau approved and issued Document No. 96 [1998] "Reply on the Peak and Valley Time Period of Small Hydropower Grid", and made it clear that on June 1, 1998, the 14-hour peak power and 10-hour valley power pricing for the large power grid would be strictly implemented from then on. Ultimately, the Taishun County Power Supply Bureau had to implement the new electricity price policy.

1.1.2 1998 to1999: The association lobbies to adjust feed-in tariffs

In the spring of 1998, due to a large amount of private capital invested in the construction of hydropower stations, there was an oversupply of electricity. The national on-grid electricity price was also adjusted to a certain extent. Many electricity price markup documents were to be discontinued by the end of 1998. And, even after the 1994 commissioning, the small hydropower feed-in tariff of 0.42–046 Yuan/kWh, which was stipulated in Document No. 433 [1998] of Zhejiang Provincial Price Bureau, was no longer implemented. In addition, the national feed-in tariff would also be reported to the Provincial Planning and Economic Commission, with the price set between 0.39 and 0.40 yuan/kWh. Upon hearing the news, the Taishun Association immediately tried to influence the price reported by the provincial planning and economic committee through various connections. He Xuchang, then executive vice president, approached Liu Xirong, then deputy secretary of the Zhejiang Provincial Party Committee. He explained the development situation and difficulties of Taishun Small Hydropower, and requested that the Zhejiang Provincial Planning and Economic Commission increase the feed-in tariff when reporting prices to the National Planning and Economic Commission. In the end, the price reported by the Zhejiang Provincial Planning and Economic Commission to the National Planning and Economic Commission was 0.45 yuan/kWh, which was 0.06 yuan/kWh higher than Jiangsu Province. "Can't underestimate this 6 cents, it's a life-saving for Taishun

Small Hydropower!", added Bao Sanchun, the then secretary-general of the Taishun County Small Hydropower Association.[1]

1.1.3 2000–2002: The Association organized petitions for fair enforcement of the price of small hydropower

Although the Taishun Small Hydropower Association won an extra 6 cents for the price of water and electricity on the grid in 1998, since 2000, the price of water and electricity in Taishun County has continuously gone down. Document No. 28 [2000] of the Wenzhou Municipal Price Bureau stipulates that the average selling price in the province was 0.5695 yuan/kWh, with the difference between purchase and sale per kWh being 0.195 yuan. In 2000, the Wenzhou Price Bureau and the Electricity Bureau issued Document No. 305 [2000], which stipulates that Taishun County would send small hydropower to Wenzhou's large network, and the peak power would be reduced from 0.65 to 0.50 yuan/kWh, with Valley power from the previous year's 0.185 yuan/kWh dropped to 0. 167 yuan/kWh. Although the province's on-grid tariff had generally decreased, Taishun County's reduction was more than twice the rate of the province's on-grid electricity price, and there were also discriminatory pricing problems due to institutional reasons. In order to obtain a fair electricity price, in early December 2000, the Taishun County Small Hydropower Association organized 105 small producers that were representative of the association's hydropower owners who then petitioned the Wenzhou municipal government for relief. They received no attention from the municipal government. When they pulled out the banner "Give us a fair and fair electricity price for small hydropower", Wu Min, who was then the vice mayor of Wenzhou, came out to receive the negotiations, but the final result of the negotiations was that the regulations of the provincial price bureau in Wenzhou could not be changed.

The next day, the Taishun County Small Hydropower Association organized the owners to petition directly to the provincial government. They had been waiting for four days before the right opportunity came—on the occasion that Premier Zhu Rongji visited Hangzhou. They put up a large sign at the entrance of the provincial government, "Give us a fair and fair electricity price for small hydropower", demanding the abolition

[1] For details, see: Cao Haidong, Power Monopoly Ice Is Hard to Break Zhejiang Private Hydropower Enterprises Struggle in Groups, Southern Weekend, 2006.09.28, http://www.southcn.com/weekend/economic/200609280037.

of the electricity Price Document No. 305 [2000] of Wenzhou Municipal Price Bureau. A secretary-general of the provincial government came out to receive and invited Wu Min, then vice mayor of Wenzhou, and Huang Zhengqiang, then magistrate of Taishun County, to coordinate and to explain. In the end, the association's representative received a reply from Wu Min, then vice mayor of Wenzhou, that "Taishun small hydropower on-grid tariff is added 5 cents per kWh". However, the final minutes of the meeting issued by Wenzhou City showed that Taishun County Small Hydropower only added 5 points to the electricity price of Wenzhou Power Grid, and the price of the Taishun County Network was not increased, and it only applied to 2000 years. He Xuchang thought this petition was imperfect, saying: "We have been deceived again!".

On May 18, 2001, the Taishun County Small Hydropower Association submitted an open letter to Zhang Dejiang, then secretary of the Zhejiang Provincial Party Committee, titled "Urgent Report on Strongly Demanding the Implementation of Guidance Prices for Fair Treatment of Taishun Small Hydropower", demanding that "the guidance prices be implemented to the letter in accordance with the principles of reasonable classification, similar prices, comprehensive balance, and comprehensive balance following Document No. 201 [2000] of Zhejiang Provincial Price Bureau". We should to adhere to the principle of "government pricing, and never allow the power supply sector to set the price of electricity". Secretary Zhang Dejiang personally instructed an investigation be instituted, and finally, Zhejiang Provincial Price Bureau issued Document No. 354 [2001] "Notice on Matters Related to Local Public Small Hydropower Feed-in Tariffs in Underdeveloped Areas", which adjusted the on-grid electricity price in Taishun County to 0.535 yuan/kWh. Though this policy was implemented from January 1, 2001, it only temporarily stabilized electricity prices for two years and was abolished at the end of 2002.

1.1.4 *From 2002 to 2006: The association cooperated with other small hydropower industry associations in the province to carry out electricity price policy negotiation*

Beginning in the fourth quarter of 2002, all the small hydropower owners worried about the 2003 on-grid tariff. The Taishun Association prepared to continue to respond but it also needed to consider how to better organize and integrate other small hydropower associations in the province to negotiate with the central provincial government departments. On December 3, 2002, under the convening of He Xuchang, executive vice president of Taishun small hydropower industry association executive vice president, 15 small hydropower association president and secretary-general in Zhejiang Province gathered in Hangzhou, to discuss the 2003 small hydropower tariff. At this meeting, the Zhejiang Small Hydropower Association was established with five organizational cores including Taishun, Tiantai, Xianju, Yongjia, and Wuyi, and He Xuchang was elected to lead the association.

Driven by the recommendations of the Taishun Association, the Zhejiang Small Hydropower Association then published its "Report on Requiring the Stabilization of the On-grid Electricity Tariff for Small Hydropower in Underdeveloped Areas" to Xi Jinping, then secretary of the Zhejiang Provincial Party Committee, and the "Proposal on Continuing to Implement Policy Support for Small Hydropower in Underdeveloped Areas" to the Provincial Price Bureau and other units. In April 2003, the third meeting of the Provincial Small Hydropower Association published its "Urgent Report on the Small Hydropower Electricity Price Problem" to the Zhejiang Provincial Price Bureau. The delegates also went to the Industrial Price Division of the Provincial Price Bureau to request stabilization of the feed-in tariff for small hydropower in less developed areas. On April 30, 2003, Document No. 159 [2003] of Zhejiang Provincial Price Bureau's "Notice on Adjusting the Maximum On-grid Tariff of Local Public Power Plants and Other Related Matters" was promulgated. It stipulated that the maximum on-grid tariff of local public small hydropower units was as follows: 0.33 yuan/kWh before the end of 1990; 0.39 yuan/kWh from 1991 to the end of 1993; 0.43 yuan/kWh between 1994 and the end of 1996; and 0.45 yuan/kWh after 1997. In 2003, power operations became subject to continuous power shortages. Coupled with drought in Taishun County, the small hydropower industry suffered great losses. The province's industrial and commercial and residential electricity prices increased, but the prices for the small hydropower grid did not increase accordingly. Considering that the existing on-grid tariff was set when there was a surplus of electricity supply in the province, the price of small hydropower on-grid also needed to be increased.

On June 2, 2004, He Xuchang convened the fourth meeting of the Provincial Small Hydropower Association. It invited Chu Dacheng, then director of the Wage and Price Division of the Price Bureau, and Ye

Zhou, then director of the Hydropower Center of the Provincial Water Resources Department, to the meeting. The association sought to influence the implementation of small hydropower prices through "influence leadership". After the meeting, they drafted its "Report on Requesting an Increase in the Province's Small Hydropower Prices" and submitted it to the Provincial Price Bureau and relevant departments. In August, the Provincial Water Resources Department also submitted to the Provincial Price Bureau its "Letter Requesting an Increase in the On-Grid Tariff for Small Hydropower" (Document No. 22 [2004]) and its "Letter on the Plan for Raising the On-Tariff for Small Hydropower" (Document No. 26 [2004]). On September 20, at the suggestion of He Xuchang, chairman of the Taishun Association, the Zhejiang Rural Hydropower Industry Association held a symposium on electricity prices for presidents of the small hydropower associations of 12 counties in underdeveloped areas of Zhejiang Province. On October 1, He Xuchang convened the five organizational core members of the Provincial Small Hydropower Association to discuss the on-grid tariff of small hydropower at the Provincial Price Bureau. They submitted the "Report on Again Requesting an Increase in the Province's Small Hydropower On-Grid Tariff". Finally, on October 20, Document No. 269 [2004] of Zhejiang Provincial Price Bureau's "Notice on Local Public Small Hydropower On-grid Tariff Matters" was issued by the Zhejiang Provincial Price Bureau. It stipulated that "the maximum on-grid tariff of local public small hydropower units put into operation before the end of 1990 would be adjusted to 0.36 yuan/kWh, from November 1, 2004". This price is increased by the then price of 0.33 yuan/kWh by 3 cents.

In mid-June 2005, the fifth meeting of the Association of Small Hydropower Associations in Underdeveloped Areas of Zhejiang Province discussed the increase of the on-grid electricity price of small hydropower and the inappropriateness of on-grid electricity prices and drafted its "Report on Increasing Efforts to Support the Province's Small Hydropower Development Electricity Price Policy". In October and mid-November of 2005, the sixth and seventh meetings of the Association of Small Hydropower Associations in Underdeveloped Areas of Zhejiang Province were held in Hangzhou. The central topic of discussion was the survival and development of small hydropower. These efforts culminated in the "Letter to Xi Jinping, Secretary of the Provincial Party Committee". After this series of actions by the Small Hydropower Association, the Zhejiang Provincial Price Bureau issued Document No. 106

[2005] "Notice on Adjusting the Maximum On-grid Tariff for Non-Provincial Unified Regulation of Local Public Hydropower Generating Units", which stipulated that "electricity price of power stations put into operation before the end of 1990 will be increased from 0.36 yuan to 0.373 yuan per kWh; from 1991 to the end of 1993, from 0.39 to 0.398 yuan; from 1994 to the end of 1996, 0.43 yuan to 0.433 yuan".

In September 2006, the eighth meeting of the Association of Small Hydropower Associations in Underdeveloped Areas of Zhejiang Province was held in Hangzhou, and the leaders of the Zhejiang Provincial Price Bureau, Water Resource Department, Hydropower Management Center, and other units were invited for discussions. The main topic was Zhejiang Province's implementation of Document No. 661 [2006] "Notice on Accelerating the Structural Adjustment of the Electric Power Industry and Promoting Healthy and Orderly Development". Jointly issued by eight ministries and commissions, including the National Development and Reform Commission, the Ministry of Water Resources and the State Electricity Regulatory Commission, the document was meant to facilitate an increase in "support for renewable energy, achieve full access to the grid for hydropower, and the same price as the grid", and better implement the renewable energy electricity price policy.

Over the next 10 years, the Taishun Association urged the county power bureau to implement this electricity price policy and thereby affect hydropower grid prices. It petitioned for the fair implementation of the small hydropower grid price. By cooperating with other small hydropower industry associations in the province, the Taishun Association was able to effectively participate in policy formation through negotiation.

1.2 Analysis of the Taishun Association's Policy Participation

1.2.1 External Environment for Policy Participation

Whether it was the support and encouragement of the laws and regulations or the relative smoothness of the informal system, the Taishun Association's external environment for the policy participation was ideal. Various preferential policies for the development of small hydropower and the reform of the on-grid tariff and small hydropower investment system laid a good legal foundation for the Taishun Association to carry out policy participation activities. From urging the Taishun County Electric Power Bureau to implement the electricity price policy to cooperating with other small hydropower associations to carry out policy negotiations with the government, the activities of Taishun small hydropower industry association all have a variety of national and provincial policy documents to support the development of small hydropower, leadership instructions as a strong backing for its policy participation.

In the incident that "urged the Taishun County Electric Power Bureau to implement the electricity price policy", the Taishun Association looked to Document No. 59 [1994] and Document No. 295 [1996] formulated by the Zhejiang Provincial Price Bureau. By their terms, the Taishun County Electric Power Bureau was required to strictly follow the policy documents of the Provincial Price Bureau. The Taishun Association was able to persuade the provincial Price Bureau to maintain policy continuity and authority. It also organized "petitions to fairly enforce the price of small hydropower on the grid" when it obtained a personal instruction from Zhang Dejiang, then secretary of the Zhejiang Provincial Party Committee, to investigate the incident.

When it came to "joint other small hydropower industry associations to hold policy negotiations with the government, the Taishun Association also effectively used Document No. 661[2006] "Notice on Accelerating the Structural Adjustment of the Electric Power Industry and Promoting Healthy and Orderly Development" jointly issued by the National Development and Reform Commission, the Ministry of Water Resources and the State Electricity Regulatory Commission, which "increased support for renewable energy, realized the full connection of hydropower and electricity, and the same price as the grid". This provision supported the Taishun Association's call for a small hydropower price policy. All these policy documents, regulations, and instructions of key leaders created a favorable external environment within which the Taishun Association could effectively operate.

1.2.2 Ability to Participate in Industry Association Policies

The Taishun Association's ability to participate in these policy events was the result of its independence, autonomy, and deft mobilization of human and other resources, despite its relative lack of financial means.

First, it was a mutually beneficial organization voluntarily formed by small hydropower owners, representing the interests of small hydropower owners. Although the Taishun Association positioned itself as a bridge and link between government departments, power enterprises, and small hydropower owners, its purpose was to represent small hydropower owners to government departments and power enterprises. And, in doing so, it fought for and coordinated the interests of its members.

Second, the president and vice president were both political elites. Shu Dingmiao, the president of the association, served as the president of the county's people's court for two terms and was quite proficient in the formulation and implementation procedures of laws and regulations. Executive Vice President He Xuchang had just retired as the director of the county poverty alleviation office. He was not only familiar with the laws and policies of the hydropower industry, but also with the rules of officialdom and policy management.

Third, the association was able to mobilize its resources. Executive Vice President He Xuchang integrated the strength of small hydropower owners in Taishun County in the early stages of establishing the Taishun Association. These owners jointly resisted the county power supply bureau's implementation of the relevant electricity price policy regulations of the provincial price bureau. He also lobbied the county government on behalf of the small hydropower owners to increase electricity prices as a means of increasing the tax revenue of the Taishun County Government. He then tried to influence the province through various relationships and organized 105 representatives of small hydropower owners to petition the Wenzhou Municipal Government and the Zhejiang Provincial Government. Given his prominence on this issue, he became the convener of the Zhejiang Small Hydropower Association. This group organized and integrated other small hydropower associations in the province to negotiate with provincial government departments to realize the goals of the small hydropower owners. Every time the provincial small hydropower friendship meeting was held, He Xuchang invited the leaders of relevant government departments to participate. This strategic effort enhanced the momentum and influence of the association. The forum discussions influenced the decision-making of the relevant governments to realize the goals of the small hydropower owners. Given his prominence, He Xuchang played a mainstay role in the policy participation of the Taishun Association. His effective resource mobilization and organization were the key to the success of the Taishun Association's policy participation.

Finally, it is clear that the Taishun Small Hydropower Industry Association is financially operating at a loss. According to the financial revenue and expenditure records of the Taishun Association from 1996 to 2003, the organization's total income was 632,858.26 yuan, yet the total expenditure was 759,057.34 yuan, with a loss of 126,199.08 yuan. Despite its success, its meager financial resources limit its policy participation activities. Also, as He Xuchang is getting old, the association cannot rely on his connections and will be like-wise limited when going forward.

1.2.3 Policy Will at Different Levels of Government

For the policy participation activities of the Taishun Association, government will at different levels was different.

First, the Taishun County Party Committee and the county government fully supported the Taishun Association's agitation for the electricity price policy change. Motivated by the county's economic development, GDP growth, and tax revenue, the Taishun County Committee of the CPC and the county government issued a series of policies to support the investment and development of small hydropower, such as Document No. 05 [1996] issued Taishun County Committee of the CPC "Several Provisions on the Ninth Five-Year Plan for Poverty Alleviation Work and Mountain Area Development", which encouraged private capital to invest. This document put forward the principle of "who invests, who owns, who benefits", and relaxed the operating period to 50 years. Document No. 20 of the Taishun County Committee of the CPC [1996] "Several Regulations on the Ninth Five-Year Plan for Poverty Alleviation and the Development of Mountainous Areas" also supported the development of hydropower resources in the form of joint-stock cooperation. It advocated for and encouraged multi-channel and multi-level investment in electricity production. It also stipulated that new hydropower stations built during the Ninth Five-Year Plan period and later would be exempt from paying water conservancy construction funds, land management fees, forest land compensation fees, and water resource fees for three years after they were put into operation.

The support of the leadership of the Taishun County Party Committee and County Government empowered the Taishun Association to repeatedly go to the Zhejiang Provincial Party Committee and Provincial Government. On the morning of March 20, 2000, the leaders of the Taishun County Government reported in detail to the Vice Governor of Zhejiang Province in charge of hydropower. Their report detailed the difficulties faced by the current development of small hydropower in Taishun County. From 21 to 22 March 2000, Xia Zhibi, executive deputy magistrate of Taishun County, together with the leaders of the Taishun County department in Hangzhou, sought similar support from the leaders of the Provincial Planning and Economic Commission, the Provincial Water Resources Department, and other departments, requesting support.

Second, departments in the Wenzhou municipal government hold a neutral attitude toward the policy participation activities of the Taishun Association. In 2000, the Wenzhou Price Bureau and the Electricity Bureau issued Document No. 305 [2000]. It stipulates that the price of small hydropower peak and valley electricity sent to Wenzhou's large network from Taishun County would be dropped, with the average peak and valley electricity price being about 0. 40 yuan/kWh. Among the electricity prices transmitted to the Wenzhou grid, the peak and valley prices of different counties and cities were also different. Among them, the Taishun transmission price was the lowest among all counties and cities. In response to this, Shu Dingmiao, president of the association, who was also a deputy to the National People's Congress, submitted a proposal to the Wenzhou Municipal People's Congress titled "Calling for the Stabilization of Taishun Small Hydropower Policy". Although the proposal was highly valued by Ruan Hui, executive vice mayor of Wenzhou, who convened the heads of the relevant departments, including Cai Yitian, director of the Wenzhou Municipal Electric Power Bureau, to discuss the issue, no substantive policy was introduced. Even when the representative of the association received a reply from Wu Min, vice mayor of Wenzhou City, that "Taishun small hydropower on-grid tariff was increased by 5 cents per kWh", in the end, the minutes of the meeting issued by Wenzhou City could not be implemented.

The relevant leaders of the Wenzhou Municipal Government paid attention to and supported the policy participation activities of the Taishun Association. But they could not provide strong policy support and guarantees. Relevant departments obstructed that for their own reasons. On the one hand, Zhejiang Province administered some counties, including Taishun, at the provincial level. The development level of small hydropower in Taishun County did not directly impact the finances of Wenzhou City. This reduced the enthusiasm of the municipal government to fully support the policy activities of the association. On the other hand, the interests of hydropower enterprises directly under the power sector caused great resistance to any effort by the Wenzhou municipal government to coordinate electricity prices on behalf of various counties and cities.

1.2.4 Strategic Interaction Between the Association and the Government

Through different stages of policy participation activities, the Taishun Association carried out positive strategic interaction with governments at all levels. These were mainly manifested in strategies such as "association resistance (petition)", "mutual compromise between the government and association", and "multi-organization cooperation". The core purpose of the Taishun Association's policy participation activities was to influence the introduction, adjustment, and implementation of the on-grid tariff policy for small hydropower. As it participated in policy events, its overall strategy was to use existing higher-level policies and regulations to win the support of important leaders of party committees and governments at all levels. This was possible because it sought to unite other small hydropower industry associations that had the same interests to form a hydropower association of these groups, achieve complementary advantages and resource sharing, as well as enhance its policy influence.

When faced with the problem of uncertain electricity prices in 2003, the Taishun Association began to take the strategic action of "multi-organization cooperation", not only uniting other small hydropower industry associations and small hydropower owners who are concerned about the small hydropower price policy, but also used the provincial small hydropower association as a platform to win over the provincial water conservancy department, the provincial price bureau, and other relevant government departments. This formed a strong partnership on the grounds of policy consultation, participation in discussions, and joint implementation of the latest national policies.

In the face of the unfairness and injustice of the electricity price policy, the Taishun Association organized small hydropower owners to carry out collective petition actions. At first, the small hydropower owners collectively petitioned the Wenzhou municipal government, but the Wenzhou municipal government ignored them. Even after being received by Wu Min, then vice mayor of Wenzhou, the Wenzhou municipal government was not able to respond effectively to its request. The Taishun Association persevered and turned to the petitioning strategy and led the small hydropower owners to petition the Zhejiang provincial government. The local government also adjusted its own behavior in time after discovering the association's alternation to petitioning strategy and adopted corresponding response strategies. The magistrate of Taishun County and relevant leaders of Wenzhou City rushed to Hangzhou overnight to try to dissuade the Taishun Association from petitioning. In the face of petitioning activities organized by the association, the Zhejiang provincial government acted as an intermediate coordinator to balance the conflicts of interest between the city and the county governments and small hydropower owners. Under the coordination of the secretary-general of the provincial government, the two sides pushed Wu Min, then vice mayor of Wenzhou, to make a "compromising" promise of "5 cents per kWh of on-grid electricity price for Taishun small hydropower". Interestingly, the promise kept turned out to be "the electricity price of Wenzhou Power Grid was only added 5 points, and the price of the Taishun County Network was not increased, and it was only valid in 2000". Although the petition failed to meet the expectations of the small hydropower owners, the Taishun Association forced relevant interest groups to make compromises and concessions.

In addition, the policy participation activities of the Taishun Association also reflected the change in interactions between the association and the government. The Taishun Association sought justice, fairness, and reasonableness for on-grid electricity prices in Taishun County. Although the association petitioned the municipal government and the provincial government to obtain the commitment of Wenzhou municipal leaders, but there has never been a formal policy document to determine and standardize, and the effect of the specific implementation is also greatly reduced. It was not until the "external informal environment" of Zhang

Dejiang, then secretary of the provincial party committee, "gave instructions and investigations", and the Zhejiang Provincial Price Bureau issued Document No. 354 [2001] "Notice on Matters Related to Local Public Small Hydropower On-grid Tariffs in Underdeveloped Areas", that the city and county governments and their relevant departments had to comply with the requirements of the "notice" to implement it, thus completely changing the interaction between the association and the county and city governments.

1.2.5 Changes in Local Government Behavior Spurred by Association Engagement

First, the policy participation of the Taishun Association led to the correction of the unreasonable and unfair behaviors of local governments, such as the delay in implementing the new electricity price policy document promulgated by the Zhejiang Provincial Price Bureau. The policy participation of the association forced the Taishun County Power Supply Bureau to implement the new electricity price policy in accordance with the requirements of the Provincial Price Bureau. Second, its policy participation gave the government a boost to positive action, such as the Zhejiang Provincial Planning and Economic Commission tried to persuade the National Planning Commission to increase the on-grid electricity prices of small hydropower in Zhejiang Province. As a result, the electricity price in Zhejiang Province is 0.06 yuan higher than that in Jiangsu Province. Third, the policy participation action of The Taishun Association has built a good platform and mechanism for benign dialogue between the government and enterprises, which is conducive to eliminating information asymmetry between the two sides and jointly discussing the formulation, implementation, and modification of policies. For example, the Zhejiang Small Hydropower Association provides a dialogue platform for the Provincial Water Conservancy Department, the Provincial Price Bureau, and other relevant government departments and small hydropower owners and other small hydropower associations, and smoothly realized the transmission of government policy intentions and the transmission of enterprise policy benefits. In summary, although the Taishun Association has failed to make government actions more transparent, legalized, and institutionalized, the association driven by the interests of members is an effective supervisory force in transforming the government into a more responsible one.

In short, the policy participation activities of the Taishun Association were proactive. First, the Taishun Association's activities were supported by the external environment, such as its support from the macro-policy environment and the instructions and encouragement of key provincial leaders. Second, the policy participation behavior of the Taishun Association was positive and effective. The fundamental conflict of interest was between the Taishun Association and the Taishun County Power Supply Bureau, the relevant power department of Wenzhou City, and other institutions. Its policy participation targets, however, were relevant departments of higher-level governments, such as the Water Conservancy Department and the Price Bureau. In face of that, the Taishun Association made use of policy documents, leaders' instructions, and the support of higher-level governments. Finally, by applying various strategies such as petition for resistance, compromise, and multi-organization cooperation, the Taishun Association launched a strategic interaction with the government and successfully achieved its purpose of policy participation.

2 Wenzhou E-commerce Industry Association Advocates, Formulates, and Implements the "1 + x, Series of Policies to Accelerate the Development of Wenzhou E-Commerce"

The "Wenzhou Model" is famous for the development of that city's private economy. After 30 years of glory, Wenzhou's economic development faced problems like labor shortage, private lending crisis, insufficient industrial land, small-scale and scattered distribution of its built environment, etc. These issues seriously restricted the development of the city's industry. Against the backdrop of ongoing transformation and upgrading of traditional industries, the development of Wenzhou's private economy urgently needed the vitality of information technology to open an era of e-commerce for traditional industries. The Wenzhou E-commerce Industry Association (hereafter Wenzhou Association) was officially established on December 27, 2011, for the purpose of better integrating and coordinating businesses and individuals in e-commerce development related with development and operations, scientific research, services and product manufacturing. The association also sought to accelerate information development and research of the Wenzhou e-commerce platform, and promote the transformation and upgrading of SMEs in Wenzhou.

Wenzhou E-commerce Industry Association is a comprehensive industry association. The association comprised mainly of unit members, with 62 individual members and 20 president and vice president units. Executive vice president units included the Wenzhou Advanced Technology Manufacturing Research Institute of Huazhong University of Science and Technology, the Wenzhou Branch of Agricultural Bank of China, the Zhejiang Baifangwang Technology Co., Ltd. Vice president units included the Wenzhou Stainless Steel Electronic Trading Center Co., Ltd., Wenzhou Research Institute of China Leather and Footwear Industry Research Institute, Wenzhou Institute of Quality and Technical Supervision and Testing, Wenzhou Leather Science and Technology Research Institute, Dean of the School of Information and Engineering, Wenzhou University Business School, Wenzhou Gongsheng Industrial Co., Ltd., China Mobile Wenzhou Branch, Wenzhou Daily, etc. The average annual income of the association was about 300,000 yuan. Most of that was made up of membership fees and service income. The association's membership fees for group units were 2000 yuan/year, and 5000 yuan/year for director units. The association's services included providing industry information, technical consulting, and vocational skills training.

The association had four full-time staff, no part-time staff. The president at the time, Chen Qingke, was the president of Tsingshan Holding Group Co., Ltd. Lin Kefu, the then secretary of the party committee of Chint Group, was the honorary president. Wang Shenghao, the then executive vice president, was the executive vice president of the Wenzhou Advanced Technology Manufacturing Research Institute of Huazhong University of Science and Technology. Ke Qianxi, the then executive vice president, was the vice president of the Wenzhou Branch of Agricultural Bank of China. Zhang Shaoqiangwei, then executive vice president, was the chairman of the Zhejiang Baifangwang Technology Co., Ltd. Cao Wangqiang, then vice president and full-time secretary-general, was the former general manager of the Wenzhou Ketuwenjiao Automation Technology Co., Ltd., and he was familiar with the research, development, and promotion of software and high-tech products. As an industry association of emerging industries, the establishment and development of the Wenzhou Association was strongly supported by the CPC Wenzhou Municipal Committee and the municipal government. The Wenzhou Economic and Information Commission, the Science and Technology Bureau, the Commerce Bureau, and the High-tech Industrial Park gave lots of policy support to the development of association. Xu Yufei, then vice mayor of Wenzhou, made important speeches to the Wenzhou E-commerce Association to show support from the government side.

2.1 Policy Participation Paths

Wenzhou's municipal government listed the e-commerce industry as a strategic emerging industry in Wenzhou. It sought to promote the transformation and upgrading of traditional industries in Wenzhou, to build an industrial platform for manufacturing informatization, circulation industry informatization and business informatization, and an information platform connecting production, learning, research, and business processes. The Wenzhou Association have successfully achieved policy participation in the following activities: "Wenzhou Two Sessions Proposal Speech", "Wenzhou E-commerce 1 + X Policy Formulation", and "the Implementation of Wenzhou E-Commerce 1234 Engineering Policies".

2.1.1 Policy Proposal by the Association's Vice President at the Meeting of the Wenzhou CPPCC

In February 2012, before the opening of the Wenzhou Two Sessions, Chen Qixian, then vice president of the Wenzhou Association, addressed the first meeting of the 10th Wenzhou CPPCC as a member. Along with presenting the Wenzhou Association's proposals, he spoke about accelerating the construction of Wenzhou's e-commerce environment and promoting the transformation and development of Wenzhou's real economy. His remarks mentioned that "Wenzhou's small and medium-sized micro enterprises mainly produce light industrial products closely related to people's lives"; "Wenzhou's products, as shown in e-commerce sales records, rank first in all regions of the province, even though the sales records for Wenzhou's e-commerce platform channels rank low in the province"; and "For these traditional industries with the 'made in Wenzhou' brand, we should promote and reposition them so they will become a sunrise industry that will never end". He concluded by acknowledging that, during the period of Wenzhou's ascendancy, many operating businesses were deluged with private capital and became "zombies" held aloft by "hot money".

The proposal advocated for listing the "e-commerce industry as a strategic emerging industry in Wenzhou, encouraging and promoting its vigorous development, establishing the core position of the e-commerce industry, and giving full play to the supporting and promoting role of e-commerce in developing traditional industries". One specific measure was constructing Wenzhou's e-commerce industrial park. Wenzhou's leaders valued the proposal. On February 22, Chen Jinbiao, then mayor of Wenzhou, instructed the Municipal Bureau of Commerce to learn from the experience of Jinhua, Hangzhou, and other places. He directed that "opinions on strengthening and promoting the development of e-commerce" should be put forward to strengthen guidance. On February 23, Chen Derong, then secretary of the Wenzhou Municipal Party Committee, instructed the Commerce Bureau and Comrade Xiang Qing, then director of the Wenzhou Municipal Bureau of Commerce, to take the lead on the "1 + X" opinion on promoting the development of e-commerce within two weeks.

2.1.2 *The Association Formulated a Series of Policies for the Development of Wenzhou E-Commerce "1 + X"*

On the afternoon of February 28, 2012, Wenzhou Municipal Bureau of Commerce invited Chen Qingke, president, and Chen Qixian, vice president, of the Wenzhou Association, as well as the organization's secretariat to discuss implementing the instructions of the secretary of the Municipal Party Committee and the mayor. At the same time, the Wenzhou Municipal Bureau of Commerce commissioned the Wenzhou Association to draft a "Framework Opinion on How to Develop Wenzhou's E-commerce Industry Economy" (the so-called "1 + X" series of policies to accelerate the development of Wenzhou's e-commerce). The first draft was presented on the morning of March 2. The Municipal Bureau of Commerce then sent the first draft to all relevant units for comments. Those comments were returned to the Wenzhou Association for adjustment and revision, before submitting it to the Wenzhou Municipal Government for approval.

On July 9, 2012, the Wenzhou Municipal People's Government Office officially released Document No. 137 [2012] "Implementation Opinions on Accelerating the Development of E-commerce (Trial)" and the annexes: "Wenzhou Promoting E-commerce", "Measures for Supporting Development", "Wenzhou Measures for Standardizing E-commerce Development", "Wenzhou E-commerce Demonstration Leading Enterprise Identification Measures", "Wenzhou Integrity E-commerce Enterprise Identification and Management Measures". This was the comprehensive document for the "1 + X" policy with the purpose of promoting e-commerce development put forward by Chen Derong, then secretary of the Wenzhou Municipal Party Committee. In this policy, "1" refers to the "Implementation Opinions on Accelerating the Development of E-commerce (Trial)", which clarifies the overall thinking, objectives, priorities, and corresponding guarantee system for the development of e-commerce in Wenzhou. The "X" refers to the four specific implementation measures: "Wenzhou Measures for Promoting E-commerce Development", "Wenzhou Measures for Standardizing E-commerce Development", "Wenzhou E-commerce Demonstration Leading Enterprise Identification Measures", and "Wenzhou Honest E-commerce Enterprise Identification and Management Measures". These implementation measures, by describing the necessary funds, land, infrastructure, support systems, and development environment, were a reiteration of Wenzhou Municipal Government's support for the development of Wenzhou's e-commerce industry. The detailed explanations were presented in terms familiar to the e-commerce industry and were meant to spotlight the dynamic management of both the cutting-edge and the leading e-commerce enterprises.

2.1.3 The Association Implements the "1234" Project Policy of E-Commerce in Wenzhou

After the official release of the "1 + X" policy document, the Wenzhou municipal government proposed the "1234" e-commerce project. Its objectives were to build a number of e-commerce headquarter buildings, to create two e-commerce industrial parks, and to build industrial electricity capacity. Three public service platforms comprised the business alliance, the public service platform, the technical support and talent training service platform, and the logistics public service platform. They were meant to improve four supporting systems: networks, credit, logistics, and publicity. They formed Wenzhou's initial e-commerce development environment and e-commerce ecological industry chain. These groups provided sound industrial policies as well as reasonable and efficient management systems. As a basic support system for a complete public service platform, these groups worked toward the overall goal of building a nationally recognized light industrial base composed of an online e-commerce city and a national e-commerce demonstration city. Encouraged and promoted by the "1234" project, the Wenzhou Association joined hands with the Wenzhou Stainless Steel Electronic Trading Center, the Wenzhou branches of the Industrial and Commercial Bank of

China, the Agricultural Bank of China, the Bank of China, the Construction Bank, and the Chouzhou Bank, as well as other e-commerce financial services enterprises and state-owned banks. The purpose was to integrate the financial, e-commerce, and logistics resources through enterprises that were committed to creating capital flow, information flow, logistics, and business flow—namely, "four streams in one" of the Wenzhou financial e-commerce public service platform.

To begin work on both the "Implementation Opinions on Further Accelerating the Upgrading and Development of the City's Commercial Market" of the Wenzhou Municipal Government and the "1234" project policy, the Wenzhou Association, the Tsingshan Holding Group, the Wenzhou Stainless Steel Electronic Trading Center Co., Ltd., and the Wenzhou Qinggang Trading Co., Ltd. formed a project implementation team to create a "Wenzhou stainless steel industry bulk commodity e-commerce public service platform". After focusing on solving the problems of distribution center and storage land of Wenzhou stainless steel commercial logistics center, the platform also attracted large credit funds from bank financing institutions to further solve the financial problem of the project. On this basis, the project team also introduced third-party quality-testing institutions and integration. This included making third-party warehousing, third-party testing, and third-party monitoring a joint force, and aggregating the terminal products and production and marketing information of the small and medium-sized enterprises in all industries into a unified data platform. From this platform, industry associations and leading enterprises could further promote the aggregation of industrial chains on a third-party platform. This was believed to be the solid foundation for the transformation and upgrading of Wenzhou's stainless steel industry. Through the creation of the "Wenzhou Stainless Steel Industry Bulk Commodity E-commerce Public Service Platform", the Wenzhou Association explored the establishment of the "Wenzhou Model" of economic development and industrial transformation through informatization and financial reform.

In addition, the Wenzhou Association often participated in meetings on e-commerce held by the municipal government and its relevant departments to jointly discuss how to further strengthen the development of e-commerce in Wenzhou or how to solve new problems in the process of development.

2.2 *Case Analysis of Policy Participation*

2.2.1 External Environment for Policy Participation

The Wenzhou Association was established by leading enterprises, with full local government support, to speed along the transformation and upgrading of traditional industries in Wenzhou. The city is well-known in China for its active and developed private economy and its dazzling number of privately established industry associations and chambers of commerce. The establishment of the Wenzhou Association was supported by the state and soon acquired its legitimacy due to the quick governmental follow-up to its policy participation activities. As an emerging strategic industry, e-commerce in Wenzhou was still in its infancy. It required effective guidance, encouragement, and standardization, all of which were supplied by the Wenzhou municipal government's policies. Therefore, the Wenzhou Association's policy participation activities were of the following types: "policy advocacy", "participation in decision-making", and "private benefit government". By participating in those ways, the association realized specific policy items in the "policy proposals of the CPPCC of the two sessions", participated in the formulation of the "1 + x series of policies for the development of Wenzhou's e-commerce" and the implementation of the "Wenzhou e-commerce '1234', project" and other operable specific policies.

In short, the macro background of Wenzhou's economic transformation provided a good external environment for the policy participation of the Wenzhou Association. Likewise, the agreement of the private enterprises, banks, and governments about the need for industrial change also provided the proper external conditions for Wenzhou Association's policy participation in the forms of technology, land, capital, and human resources.

2.2.2 Policy Participation Ability of the Wenzhou Association

Wenzhou Association's ability to participate in policy is mainly reflected in its autonomy, human resources, and resource mobilization.

First, Wenzhou Association was initiated by leading enterprises in the industry, and has the most detailed and complete grasp of the market space and development planning of Wenzhou's e-commerce industry. As a newly established industry association, its business activities, funding sources, and personnel arrangements were completely independent of the government. Its strong autonomy also ensured that the association truly represented the interests of member companies.

Second, in terms of human resource advantages, Wenzhou Association recruited talents familiar with industry development. Then President Chen Qingke was the president of the Tsingshan Holding Group Co., Ltd., which provided capital and technical support for the association's policy participation. Cao Wangqiang, then vice president and full-time secretary-general, was the former general manager of the Wenzhou Ketuwenjiao Automation Technology Co., Ltd. He was familiar with the research and development and promotion of software and high-tech products in the e-commerce industry, thereby ensuring the implementation of the association's policy participation. As one of the founders of the association, Chen Qixian, then vice president of the association, was the director of the research committee of the Wenzhou Municipal Committee of the Democratic Construction Association. His involvement provided a smooth channel for the association to carry out policy advocacy activities supported by the government for the development of Wenzhou's e-commerce industry. He also delivered the association's proposals to the two sessions and obtained important instructions from the mayor and secretary of the Wenzhou municipal party committee.

Finally, in terms of resource mobilization, due to the comprehensiveness, complexity, and cross-regional nature of the development of Wenzhou's e-commerce industry, Wenzhou Association fully mobilized resources from all parties in the process of policy participation. It skillfully integrated the resources of enterprises, research institutions, financial institutions, and media for the development of the e-commerce industry, such as when formulating and implementing the "1 + X series of policies for the development of Wenzhou e-commerce". The Wenzhou Association then applied its knowledge to other industries such as clothing, shoe leather, glasses, electrical appliances, and other traditional industries in Wenzhou and integrated them into the public service platform of the Human Industry E-commerce Alliance. It also relied on several universities and research institutes to build a public service platform for technical support and talent training for the development of Wenzhou's e-commerce industry. They included Wenzhou University, Wenzhou Leather Science and Technology Research Institute, the School of Information and Engineering of Wenzhou Medical College, Wenzhou Advanced Technology Manufacturing Research Institute of Huazhong University of Science and Technology, as well as e-commerce technology service enterprises such as Zhejiang Baifangwang Technology Co., Ltd. and Wenzhou Gongsheng Industrial Co., Ltd. Wenzhou Association also coordinated the assistance of various county- and district-level governments and the administrative committee of the municipal high-tech zone. They were responsible for the implementation of land for the construction of e-commerce headquarters buildings and e-commerce industrial parks, while the Wenzhou Municipal Bureau of Commerce and the Municipal Economic and Information Commission were responsible for implementing the construction of the e-commerce application network system and logistics distribution system, and the Municipal Administration for Industry and Commerce, the Commerce Bureau, and the Publicity Department of CPC Wenzhou Municipal Committee were responsible for implementing the construction of e-commerce creditworthiness, network security system and publicity and promotion system.

2.2.3 The Policy Will of the Wenzhou Municipal Government

One great support for Wenzhou's industry associations has always been the Wenzhou municipal government. The city supported the rise and development of its e-commerce industry because doing so was conducive to the transformation and upgrading of Wenzhou's traditional industries, and to the increase of Wenzhou municipal government's funding from the private economy's tax revenue. The Wenzhou Municipal Government's support for the Wenzhou Association's policy engagement activities differed at different stages.

First, in the policy advocacy stage, Chen Jinbiao, then mayor of Wenzhou, and Chen Derong, then secretary of the CPC Wenzhou Municipal Committee, highly praised and gave important instructions on Wenzhou Association's proposal, "Suggestions on Accelerating the Construction of E-commerce Ecological Chain and Promoting the Transformation and Development of Wenzhou's Real Economy" submitted by Chen Qixian, then vice president of the association. It is this proposal that led to the instructions requiring the Municipal Bureau of Commerce to take the lead in implementing the proposal. That action enabled the Wenzhou Association to draft the Wenzhou e-commerce Development Plan policy, which shows that the association's proposal played an important role in Wenzhou's economic transformation and development.

Second, in the policy formulation stage, the association was fully entrusted by the Wenzhou Municipal Bureau of Commerce to draft and formulate the "1 + X, series of policies for the development of e-commerce in Wenzhou", which were officially issued as a document of the Wenzhou Municipal Government Office. Since most of the policy content is formulated by the association, the association is well placed to realize the will of the industry and the interests of its members in government policy documents.

Finally, in the policy implementation stage, the government allows the Wenzhou Association to undertake the platform construction work and give corresponding supporting funds and implementation powers, such as to build the "Wenzhou Financial e-commerce Public Service Platform" and "Wenzhou Stainless Steel Industry Bulk Commodity E-commerce Public Service Platform" to better implement some of the policies of Wenzhou's e-commerce "1234" Project.

2.2.4 *Strategic Interaction Between the Association and the Government*

From submitting the policy proposal, drafting and formulating the 1 + x policy, and implementing the e-commerce 1234 policy, the Wenzhou Association and the Wenzhou Municipal Government achieved win–win cooperation, showing the features of "acquiescence or compliance" and "adoption or control".

On the one hand, the Wenzhou Association's "acquiesce or compliance" strategy enhanced its legitimacy. This led to the provision of government resources through the "political marriage" of the two groups in this policy area. In December 2011, the newly established Wenzhou Association was ready to open up new resource development channels. The "Two Sessions Proposal" presented in February 2012 was the newly established association's first action to draw the government's attention. Using the CPPCC channel, the association directly made its case for obtaining government resources. It resulted in the crucial instructions of the secretary of the Wenzhou Municipal Party Committee and the mayor. With the policy formulation tasks entrusted by the Commerce Bureau, the Wenzhou Association integrated the ideas, concepts, planning goals, and key tasks of the development of the e-commerce industry into the policy documents of the government. This created the foundation for government policy support for the follow-up work of the association.

On the other hand, in response to the Wenzhou Association's "acquiescence or compliance" strategy, the Wenzhou Municipal Government adopted a "manipulation" strategy. The government was not familiar with the e-commerce industry. CPC Wenzhou Municipal Committee, Wenzhou Municipal Government and the Wenzhou Municipal Bureau of Commerce hoped that the association would become the government's policy arm for the development of the e-commerce industry. This was an example of the "Adoption" and the "Influence and Control" strategies. The association would be guided to promote the development of Wenzhou's e-commerce industry in accordance with the government's intentions to better serve Wenzhou's economic transformation. For example, the secretary of the CPC Wenzhou Municipal Committee and the mayor made a positive response to the "two sessions of the proposal" made by the vice president of Wenzhou Association, and asked the Wenzhou Municipal Bureau of Commerce to take the lead in implementing the proposal, while the Wenzhou Municipal Bureau of Commerce not only "adopted" Wenzhou Association into the process of Wenzhou e-commerce policy development, but also give the association the right to implement e-commerce policies and build a comprehensive platform.

2.2.5 *Changes in Local Government Behavior Spurred by Association Engagement*

First, the policy advocacy of the Wenzhou Association helped push the development of the city's e-commerce industry onto the policy agenda of the Wenzhou Municipal Government. Long before the official announcement of the association's establishment, the relevant person in charge was planning ways to influence the government to put the development of the e-commerce industry on the policy agenda. Despite these plans, the policy had not attracted the attention of Wenzhou's higher-level leadership. In December 2011, after the official announcement of the establishment of the Wenzhou Association, the relevant responsible persons pointed to the association's mission as indicative of the correct policy direction. They advocated that the government introduce e-commerce industry development policies as soon as possible with the help of the media's publicity on the significance of the establishment of the association at the time of the association's establishment. In February 2012, during the "Two Sessions", the CPPCC proposal was used as a channel to submit a proposal for the development of e-commerce industry. At that time, Chen Jinbiao was elected to be the mayor of Wenzhou. The pressure to transform traditional industries in Wenzhou made the development of the local economy more urgent for the city's government. The proposal by the association's vice president at the CPPCC met the new mayor's need of political achievements. In other words, the "policy window" was open. In the end, reading the political signal correctly, the secretary of the CPC Wenzhou Committee and the mayor both gave instructions to develop the Wenzhou e-commerce industry and set the agenda for policies.

Second, the Wenzhou Association promoted cooperation with the Wenzhou Municipal Government to take part in the government's policy formulation and implementation. It is not uncommon for the government to cooperate with industry associations and chambers of commerce to provide public services or public goods. Governments often purchase the services of industry associations and chambers of commerce and entrust them to formulate annual industrial development reports and industry standards. However, there are few examples of local governments that have fully delegated authority to industry associations and chambers of commerce to draft policy documents and publish them for implementation in official municipal documents. In the face of strategic emerging industries, the Wenzhou Municipal Bureau of Commerce knew little about the e-commerce industry. The government needed other social institutions to carry out thorough research on Wenzhou's e-commerce industry and suggest policies. At that time, the Wenzhou Association was very familiar with the development of e-commerce industry. It made itself the best cooperation object due to its successful policy advocacy. It also formulated the entirety of the "1 + X, series of policies to accelerate the development of Wenzhou e-commerce". Much thanks to its being an association of well-known professionals, and the good trust mechanism formed between the association and the government in the process of policy formulation, the foundation was laid for the government to authorize the association to carry out policy implementation. When proposing the implementation of the e-commerce "1234" project, the Wenzhou Municipal Government directly entrusted the Wenzhou Association to build the "Wenzhou Financial E-commerce Public Service Platform" and "Wenzhou Stainless Steel Industry Bulk Commodity E-commerce Public Service Platform".

In short, the policy engagement activities of the Wenzhou Association were successful. Through policy advocacy, it seized the opportunity presented by a good external environment. Industrial transformation requires the great development of strategic emerging industries. These met the needs of the Wenzhou Municipal Government's economic transformation and development. Because of this alignment, it obtained the instructions of the secretary of the Wenzhou Municipal Party Committee and the mayor to the Wenzhou Municipal Bureau of Commerce. Second, the Wenzhou Association had the skill to organize among the government's member units and then mobilized the scientific research institutes, news media, e-commerce enterprises, and other forces. It was able to pool wisdom and coordinate efforts to shape e-commerce industry policies. With its expertise, it has won the approval and decentralization of key government leaders. Finally, the interaction strategies employed by the Wenzhou Association and the city's government were effective. The association obtained the attention of Wenzhou's key leaders through media reports at the time of its establishment and its proposal to the CPPCC, among other signals. In response, the Wenzhou Municipal Bureau of Commerce employed the "Acquiescence or Compliance" and "Adoption and Manipulation" strategies. In the end, the policies introduced were in line with the wishes of the Association. After establishing a good relationship of trust with the government, the association undertook and implemented the construction of two major public service platforms, successfully achieving the purpose of its policy participation.

3 The Shanghai Indoor Environment Purification Industry Association's Successful Advocacy for the "Shanghai Air Purification Engineering Professional Contracting Enterprise Qualification Certification"

Located at the entrance of the Yangtze River Delta, Shanghai is China's economic and financial center. Creating a healthy and comfortable urban living environment for its residents is essential to enhancing Shanghai's image as an international metropolis. In the second half of 2001, China's national government issued the Indoor Air Quality Standards in response to the public's indoor air quality concerns. Catalyzed by regulation and markets' demand, Shanghai's indoor environment purification industry developed rapidly. And, in 2002, the Indoor Governance Branch of Shanghai Environmental Protection Industry Association was established, with the purpose of better regulating the industry market, investigating the current situation of the industry, helping enterprises to develop the market, and carrying out industry knowledge dissemination and protection of the legitimate rights and interests of consumers.

On August 22, 2006, the group formally became "Shanghai Indoor Environment Purification Association", and then, in 2008, it was officially renamed the "Shanghai Indoor Environment Purification Industry Association (hereafter Shanghai Association)".

The Shanghai Association is a non-profit social group voluntarily formed by enterprises engaged in the cleaning and purification industry and other related industries. The association is governed by its general assembly and council. It also has a secretariat, office staff, a membership service department, a training education department, a standardization committee, etc. At the time of this study, the association had more than 200 members, most of which were purification and cleaning enterprises for the household or the factory cleaning market. These included manufacturers, sellers, design/construction companies, consulting/service companies, etc. In 2013, the annual income of the association was 21, 070,000 yuan, with expenditures of 20,590,000 yuan. The membership fee collection rate was 82%. Membership fees accounted for 32.4% of its income, and 65% was earned by providing services to members. Other revenue accounted for 2.6%. Daily administrative expenses were only 28.1% of the association's expenditures. The association had 10 daily staff, including 8 full-time staff, all of whom had no government work experience. Wang Fang, then secretary-general, presided over the daily work of the association. As an intermediary organization, the association assisted the government in industry management. With serving the industry, industry self-discipline, and industry coordination as its basic functions, the Association protects the legitimate rights and interests of members, improves the overall quality of industry associations, and protects the legitimate rights and interests of consumers.

3.1 Policy Participation Paths

With the advancement of science and technology and the improvement of social public health requirements, Shanghai's air clean engineering market has formed a scale, and the demand for purification engineering professional construction enterprises is increasing. The professional contracting enterprise qualification standards issued by the Ministry of Construction, however, do not have this specialty. Thus, Tongji University, Jiaotong University, and other institutions with strong technical advantages have become an intermediate medium for foreign enterprises to serve. At that time, the number of Shanghai professional air purification engineering enterprises was less than 200, and Shanghai positioned its industrial development in modern service industry and modern manufacturing. For example, the microelectronics and biomedical industry output 60% of the capacity of the country. Therefore, a large number of high cleanliness requirements of plant construction and later maintenance formed a huge indoor environment clean market, yet most of the air purification projects were contracted by Engineering companies outside of Shanghai.

After confirming that the above phenomenon is the general interest and common problem of enterprises in the industry, the Shanghai Indoor Environment Purification Industry Association carried out policy participation activities such as "advocating and recommending the Shanghai Municipal Government and relevant departments to establish 'air purification engineering professional contracting enterprise qualification certification' promptly", "assisting the Shanghai Municipal Construction Management Office in demonstrating the establishment of clean qualifications and establishing regulations", and "assessing and issuing clean qualifications on behalf of administrative licenses".

3.1.1 The association advocates the establishment of "Shanghai air purification engineering professional contracting enterprise qualification certification"

In 2006, Wang Fang, then secretary-general of the Shanghai Association, submitted a proposal titled "Establishing the Qualification of Professional Contracting Enterprise for Air Purification Engineering". He did so in his capacity as a member of the Environmental Committee of the Shanghai Peasants' and Workers' Party and a member of the city's Yangpu District's CPPCC. Although it went through the channels of the CPPCC, the proposal was rejected. However, the association did not give up its policy advocacy efforts. Instead, it sent its proposal to the Shanghai Municipal Government, the Construction Commission, and other relevant departments. Using these channels, it sought to accelerate the establishment of the "certification of professional contracting enterprises for air purification engineering" in Shanghai. At first and for some time thereafter, the Shanghai Municipal Government and all the others adopted an attitude of evasion or acted as if they had not received the proposal.

On May 26, 2008, Song Yiqiao, then vice chairman of the Shanghai Municipal Committee of the Chinese People's Political Consultative Conference and president of the Shanghai Modern Service Industry Federation, convened the heads of 50 industry associations related to the modern service industry in Shanghai. The purpose was to convene during the mayor's meeting on the development of the modern service industry. For Yu Yulong, then president of the Shanghai Association, this was another opportunity for advocating the "certification of professional contracting enterprises for air purification engineering". So at this mayor's meeting on industry development, he reported the industry research report on this, and after the meeting, he also asked Song Yiqiao, vice chairman of Shanghai CPPCC, to convey the association's demands to the relevant departments. On June 4, 2008, the association again submitted a letter to Vice Chairman Song Yiqiao on "the difficulties encountered by Shanghai Indoor Environment Purification Association in solving the qualification problem of enterprise air purification engineering professional contracting enterprises". Song Yiqiao promised to give this letter to Han Zheng, then mayor of Shanghai, who responded with instructions. Previously, the Shanghai Urban and Rural Construction and Transportation Committee was uninterested in this issue. Han's instructions stated that one of the functional agency of the Shanghai Urban and Rural Construction and Transportation Commission—The Shanghai Construction Industry Management Office—should take the initiative to contact the association.

On June 27, 2008, personnel from the Shanghai Association were invited to the Shanghai Construction Industry Management Office to discuss the "qualification of professional contracting enterprises for air purification engineering". They discussed the urgency and legality of the issue of "certifying professional contracting enterprises for air purification engineering" in Shanghai, as well as the corresponding laws and regulations. According to the Shanghai Municipal Construction Industry Management Office, although it is feasible in terms of laws and regulations, sufficient research materials and data materials would be needed to fully and thoroughly demonstrate the necessity of establishing mandatory qualifications in Shanghai.

3.1.2 The association holds research discussions and submits reports regarding qualifications for the city's air purification engineering professionals

Beginning in the second half of 2008, the Shanghai Association organized several demonstrations and research events to establish the demonstration and investigation process of "clean qualifications", including conference room symposiums and on-site research seminars. The conference room discussions were conducted between enterprise personnel and the leaders of relevant departments. This was meant to provide the leaders of the Shanghai Construction Industry Management Office with a better understanding of the needs and difficulties faced by enterprises who sought to establish the "clean qualifications". Many entrepreneurs argued that Shanghai must issue the qualification of professional contracting enterprises for air purification projects, for if not, many businesses in Shanghai would not care to undertake the expense of air purification. Without certification, even those air purification businesses with a strong track record would not be able to participate in bidding events because they do not even have the qualifications. At these seminars, the Shanghai Association invited the leaders of the Shanghai Construction Industry Management Office and the Vice Chairman of the CPPCC, Song Yiqiao, to attend these meetings and learn about the needs of businesses and the "clean qualifications" issue. Whether in a conference room seminar or an on-site research discussion, at the end of each investigation, the Shanghai Association would always draft a research and discussion report, which it then submitted to the leaders of the Construction Industry Management Office. It also sent a copy to Vice Chairman Song Yiqiao, who was always concerned about the progress of the issue and had attended an on-site discussion meeting.

While organizing and carrying out the demonstration and investigation of "clean qualification", the Shanghai Association began to sort out the standards for "clean qualifications". These included the preparation principles, reference regulations, interpretation of standard terms, etc. In particular, we have carried out preparatory work for the professional training of "industrial cleaners' job qualification training". This provided the technical standards and operational solutions for the "clean qualifications".

3.1.3 The Shanghai Association is granted the pilot program "Shanghai air purification engineering professional contracting enterprise ability assessment"

In 2009, based on the feasibility of laws and regulations examined in the discussions and symposiums, the Shanghai Association made further systematic preparations for the specific implementation of its policy. First, it trained professional and technical personnel in the cleaning industry. This was the first such training in the country. Second, to develop clean technology and product standards, the association participated in the development of a series of standards such as the conversion of international standard ISm4644 into the national standard SAC/TC319. Third, it examined possible energy savings initiatives. China's clean plant energy consumption is comparatively large. China's clean plant energy consumption is more than 3 times that of Japan, Germany, and other countries. Clean workshops in China consume 15 times the energy five-star hotels. Enterprises with clean rooms were the prime targets for the energy savings initiatives.

In February 2010, the Shanghai Municipal Construction Industry Administration Office prepared to issue a "clean qualification assessment" policy after the two sessions. However, in 2010, some major construction safety incidents, such as the collapse of the "Lianhua Riverside Jingyuan" in Shanghai (also known as the "Shanghai Downing Case"), and the importance of other construction and property-related policies, led to the policy being shelved. To accelerate the introduction and implementation of this policy, the Shanghai Association immediately submitted its "Letter on Requesting Support for the Implementation and Explanation of the Trial Measures for the Capability Assessment of Shanghai Clean Engineering Professional Contracting Enterprises" to the Shanghai Municipal Construction Industry Management Office. Although there was still a gap in administrative legality between the "ability assessment of clean engineering professional contracting enterprises" and "qualification certification of air purification engineering professional contracting enterprises", the letter was an important step in the implementation of the policy.

In June 2010, the Shanghai Municipal Construction Industry Administration Office issued a reply letter on the explanation of the trial measures of the "Shanghai Clean Engineering Professional Contracting Enterprise Capacity Assessment" (Document No. 28 [2010]): "It is agreed in principle that the Shanghai Indoor Environment Purification Industry Association will pilot the 'Shanghai Air Purification Engineering Professional Contracting Enterprise Capacity Assessment', and the enterprise shall apply to the association for the ability assessment on a voluntary basis".

3.1.4 *The association will issue the "Shanghai Air Purification Engineering Professional Contracting Enterprise Qualification" certification certificate on behalf of the administrative license*

At the beginning of 2014, with the support and guidance of the relevant administrative departments, the Shanghai Association was authorized to set up a professional engineering (air purification) contracting enterprise qualification sub-project. On February 14, the Shanghai Association submitted the "Report on the Implementation Plan of the Qualification of Special Professional Engineering (Air Purification) to the Shanghai Construction Industry Management Office", which elaborated on the systematic preparation for the specific implementation of the project. This included the establishment of the organizational structure, the review office, and review working group that would be responsible for reviewing and enterprise submissions. Yu Yulong, then president and secretary of the party branch, was responsible for supervising the work of the review office. Wang Fang, then vice president and secretary-general, was the director of the review office, and was responsible for the overall review and management of its operations. Li Hong of the Ministry of Education was trained as the deputy director of the review office and was responsible for the specific review work.

The association was equipped with experts and assistants to participate in daily professional and technical review work. It purchased office equipment, revamped the association's website, published electronic newsletters, and set up a special area to timely release relevant information. It then set out to strengthen industry norms. It began by "starting from the profession, in various aspects such as professional ability review, professional and technical personnel training, dynamic professional and technical management of engineering construction, etc. The association made industry specifications for enterprises, such as enterprises applying for the engineering (air purification) contracting qualifications. Only after obtaining at least one construction qualification and the corresponding level of safety production license could an applicant apply to the association for the air purification qualification". The association also set up qualification requirements for enterprise applications: "enterprises must provide true, accurate, and complete enterprise credit information to the review office in accordance with relevant provisions". It also began supervising industry trends: "certified enterprises must undergo an annual on-site expert review by the Evaluation Office and accept industry dynamic supervision". It also set maintenance standards for the qualification: "if the enterprise no longer meets the corresponding conditions, it shall be ordered to make corrections within a time limit, and if it does not change within the time limit, its qualification certificate shall be withdrawn and reported to the municipal business acceptance center for the record".

Finally, the association directly issued the "Shanghai Air Purification Engineering Professional Contracting Enterprise Qualification" license according to the assessment results of the "Shanghai Air Purification Engineering Professional Contracting Enterprise Capacity Assessment". In other words, in the past, when an enterprise applied for the "Shanghai Air Purification Engineering Professional Contracting Enterprise Qualification" license, it first needed to obtain the assessment materials of "Shanghai Air Purification Engineering Professional Contracting Enterprise Capability" through various channels, and then submit an application for review to the Shanghai Construction Industry Management Office. Going forward, an enterprise only had to go to the association to apply. The association was made responsible for unified education and training. After passing the appraisal and review, the association directly issued the qualification certificates and then submitted it to the Construction Committee for the record.

As of 2014, the Shanghai Association had issued a total of 44 "Shanghai Air Purification Engineering Professional Contracting Enterprise Qualification" certificates, which has effectively improved the construction technology and management capabilities of air purification projects in Shanghai.

3.2 Case Analysis of Policy Participation

3.2.1 External Environment for Policy Participation

The external environment in which the Shanghai Association participated was complex and changing. It contended with a lack of policies and regulations from the Ministry of Housing and Urban-Rural Development, instructions from the Shanghai mayor, changes in policy implementation during the two sessions, and the General Office of CPC Shanghai Municipal Committee issued Document No. 19 [2011] "Guiding Opinions on Further Strengthening the Construction of Social Organizations in the City". In this environment, the policy participation activities of the Shanghai Association present three different types of "policy advocacy", "participation and decision-making", and "private government". First, there was the establishment of the "Shanghai Air Purification Engineering Professional Contracting Enterprise Qualification Certification". Second, there was investigation through discussions and symposiums for the "Shanghai Air Purification Engineering Professional Contracting Enterprise Qualification". Third, the "Shanghai Air Purification Engineering Professional Contracting Enterprise Capacity Assessment" was launched as a pilot program to issue the "Shanghai Air Purification Engineering Professional Contracting Enterprise Qualification" as the administrative license authority.

Due to the lack of qualification standards for professional contracting enterprises from the Ministry of Housing and Urban-Rural Development and the demand among Shanghai's professional construction enterprises for purification engineering, the Shanghai Association advocated for the establishment of "Shanghai Air Purification Engineering Professional Contracting Enterprise Qualification Certification". At first, this initiative was largely ignored by the Shanghai Municipal Government and relevant functional departments. The relevant functional departments adopted an evasive attitude or did not reply to the Shanghai Association's policy advocacy. Song Yiqiao, then vice chairman of the Shanghai Municipal Committee of the CPPCC, became a key figure in promoting the introduction of the policy of "Shanghai Air Purification Engineering Professional Contracting Enterprise Qualification". Through Song Yiqiao, the initiative of the Shanghai Association to establish the "Shanghai Air Purification Engineering Professional Contracting Enterprise Qualification Certification" was approved by the then Shanghai mayor, Han Zheng. Once these political orders were issued, the Shanghai Construction Industry Management Office was willing to launch the policy agenda of "Shanghai Air Purification Engineering Professional Contracting Enterprise Qualification Certification".

However, just when the Shanghai Construction Industry Management Office was about to issue and implement the policy of "Shanghai Air Purification Engineering Professional Contracting Enterprise Qualification", there was a "building collapse incident". Policy priority and urgency limited the introduction of the policy of "Shanghai Air Purification Engineering Professional Contracting Enterprise Qualification". The Shanghai Association was therefore made available and prepared to launch the relevant pilot program in the industry. In 2011, the General

Office of CPC Shanghai Municipal Committee issued the Guiding Opinions on Further Strengthening the Construction of Social Organizations in the City (Document No. 19 [2011]), which enhanced the important position of social organizations in Shanghai's economic and social development. Taking the guidance as an opportunity, the Shanghai Association negotiated with the relevant competent authorities. In accordance with the requirements of the guidance on undertaking the transfer of government functions and exercising government industry management functions, the association assessed and issued the "Shanghai Air Purification Engineering Professional Contracting Enterprise Qualification" for administrative license purposes.

3.2.2 Ability to Participate in Association Policies

The ability of the Shanghai Association to participate in these policy actions was mainly reflected in the association's strong member interests, human resources, financial resources, and external resources mobilization.

First, the Shanghai Association initiated the policy advocacy action, the "Shanghai Air Purification Engineering Professional Contracting Enterprise Qualification Certification", based on the interests of member enterprises. The demand for professional construction enterprises of purification engineering in Shanghai's air clean engineering market was increasing, but purification engineering enterprises in Shanghai was not professionally qualified to undertake air purification projects in Shanghai or in other provinces or cities, despite the city's strong technical advantages of its universities such as Tongji University and Jiaotong University. To expand the membership scope and confirm the industry's interest, the association submitted a proposal to the Shanghai Municipal Construction and Transportation Commission in which it stated that the "Shanghai Municipal Construction and Transportation Commission, according to market demand, should set up professional qualifications for air purification engineering"; "The establishment method can refer to the measures of Jiangsu Province and Shandong Province"; and, the "Shanghai Indoor Environment Purification Association is willing to do auxiliary work to assist the construction committee in plant clean indoor environmental assessment, and technical issues such as the training of employees of clean engineering enterprises".

Second, in terms of human resource advantages, Yu Yulong, then president and secretary of the party committee of the Shanghai Association, was responsible for supervising the work of the association and had certain contacts and exchanges with the Shanghai Municipal Party Committee and the Municipal Government. It was Yu Yulong, the president, who contacted Song Yiqiao, then vice chairman of the Shanghai Municipal Committee of the CPPCC and the president of the Shanghai Modern Service Industry Federation, that put the "Shanghai Air Purification Engineering Professional Contracting Enterprise Qualification" policy on the fast track for formulation and implementation. Wang Fang, vice president and secretary-general, was responsible for the daily affairs of the association and served as a member of the Environmental Committee of the Shanghai Municipal Committee of the Peasants' and Workers' Party. He was also a member of the Yangpu District Political Consultative Conference. He submitted the "Shanghai Air Purification Engineering Professional Contracting Enterprise Qualification Policy Proposal" through the channels of the CPPCC. The rest of the association's professional and technical staff assisted in daily professional and technical work. All of these efforts laid a solid technical foundation for the association to implement the assessment and issue the "Shanghai Air Purification Engineering Professional Contracting Enterprise Qualification".

Third, in terms of financial resources, the Shanghai Association had considerable income. Taking 2011 as an example, the total income in 2011 was 1,131,909 yuan. Dues collected were 376,295 yuan, accounting for about 33.2% of the total income. The government provided 50,000 yuan from the purchase of services, accounting for about 4.4%; paid service for members was 469,564 yuan, accounting for about 41.5%; training recipients 233,200 yuan, accounting for about 20.6% of the total income; other recipients were 2850 yuan, accounting for about 0.3% of the total income. Total expenditure of the association in 2011 was 1,105,633 yuan. Of this amount, expenditure on operational activities was 467,169 yuan, accounting for about 42.3%;payroll expenses are 381,719 yuan, accounting for about 34.5%; total office management costs 256,745 yuan, accounting for about 23.2%. In terms of the composition of the income, the association's 62.1% or more of the recipients came from paid member services and training services, and the government purchased services also accounted for 4.4%. In the total expenditure component, expenditure on operational activities accounted for the largest share, at 42.3%, which provides a strong financial basis for the association to conduct its business activities effectively.

Finally, the association was able to mobilize its resources, including member enterprises, technical experts and scholars, and some government officials. It coordinated these groups to promote the introduction and implementation of the "Shanghai Air Purification Engineering Professional Contracting Enterprise Qualification". This happened, for example, when the association began advocating for the establishment of the "Shanghai Air Purification Engineering Professional Contracting Enterprise Qualification Certification". The association mobilized resources such as CPPCC proposals, the mayor's conference speech reports, and CPPCC Vice Chairman Song Yiqiao presentation. During the demonstration and research stage when the association organized discussions and symposiums for the "Shanghai Air Purification Engineering Professional Contracting Enterprise Qualification" policy, member enterprises provided on-site investigation sites, allowing enterprises to speak for themselves. This allowed the members to put forward the establishment of "clean qualifications" to government officials to visit projects on-site. These efforts ultimately lead to the association taking the technical lead during the pilot stage of the "Shanghai Air Purification Engineering Professional Contracting Enterprise Capacity Assessment" and was named the official assessment organization for newly created "Shanghai Air Purification Engineering Professional Contracting Enterprise Qualification".

3.2.3 *The Policy Willingness of the Shanghai Municipal Government and the Municipal Construction Industry Management Office for the Policy Participation Activities of the Shanghai Association*

The Shanghai Municipal Construction Industry Administration Office (under the Shanghai Urban and Rural Construction and Transportation Commission) revealed different levels of policy intentions at different stages in this case study. This alternation is largely highlighted by the fact that the Shanghai Construction Industry Management Office, as a functional department of the government, needed the instructions of important leaders in the municipal and party hierarchy and had to demonstrate that the newly introduced policies were legal. On this basis, the Shanghai Construction Industry Administration Office issued a policy and delegated authority to the Shanghai Association to implement the policy.

First, in the early stage of the association's policy advocacy, the Shanghai Urban and Rural Construction and Transportation Committee adopted an evasive attitude, not replying to the association's policy advocacy. It pursued the principle of "less is better than more and none is better than less" to avoid opening new administrative businesses. In 2006, Wang Fang, secretary-general of the Shanghai Association, submitted its proposal "On the Establishment of Qualification Certification of Air Purification Engineering Professional Contracting Enterprises" as a member of the Environmental Committee of the Shanghai Peasants' and Workers' Party and a member of the Yangpu District CPPCC. Despite these political connections, it did not receive attention from relevant departments and the qualification proposals and plans submitted by the association through many channels later were all lost.

Second, Song Yiqiao, vice chairman of the Shanghai Municipal Committee of the CPPCC and president of the Shanghai Modern Service Industry Federation, reversed the "inaction" of the Shanghai municipal government and its relevant departments to the impetus for the "clean qualification" policy. In June 2008, Song Yiqiao sent the letter "Shanghai Indoor Environment Purification Association in Solving the Qualification Problems of Enterprise Air Purification Engineering Professional Contracting Enterprises" to the leaders of the Shanghai Municipal Party Committee and Municipal Government. Under the instructions of Han Zheng, then mayor of Shanghai, the Shanghai Construction Industry Administration Office took the initiative to call the Shanghai Association to discuss the legal aspects of "clean qualification", as well as the implementation of standards and technology development.

Finally, the Shanghai Municipal Construction Industry Management Office entrusted the Shanghai Association to carry out the "Shanghai Air Purification Engineering Professional Contracting Enterprise Qualification Certification" program. Based on the results of the association's early pilot, in early 2014, the Shanghai Construction Industry Management Office officially entrusted the association to issue the "Shanghai Air Purification Engineering Professional Contracting Enterprise Qualification" on behalf of the administrative license. This step was of great significance in the history of the air purification industry and engineering construction subcontracting in Shanghai and even the whole country.

3.2.4 *Strategic interactions between the association and the government*

The Shanghai Association's positive and effective strategic interactions with the Shanghai Municipal Government and relevant functional departments were revealed by the policy advocacy around the "Shanghai Air Purification Engineering Professional Contracting Enterprise Qualification Certification", the demonstration and research discussions before the introduction of the policy, the pilot implementation of the "Shanghai Air Purification Engineering Professional Contracting Enterprise Capacity Assessment", and the association-issued "Shanghai Air Purification Engineering Professional Contracting Enterprise Qualification" on behalf of the administrative licensure authority. These strategies were "government avoidance", "association acquiescence or compliance", and "government adopt or control".

The Shanghai Association adopted a "compliance" strategy in "acquiescence or compliance" to enhance the legitimacy of the association's policy participation. In the process of policy advocacy, the association did not collectively petition member enterprises to express their interests, but delivered policy suggestions through multiple channels. Even in the case of unsuccessful policy advocacy, the association was disciplined and overcame its difficulties. To solve the qualification problem, the association sought out Song Yiqiao, then vice chairman of the Shanghai Municipal Committee of the CPPCC who interacted with the Shanghai municipal leaders. The association's "acquiescence or compliance" strategy eventually won itself the image of "obedience", "non-trouble making", and "aiming at solving problems" in the minds of government departments, and thus strengthened the legitimacy of the association's policy advocacy. Its proposal, "On the Establishment of Shanghai Enterprise Air Purification Engineering Professional Contracting Enterprise Qualification", was submitted to the Shanghai Construction Industry Management Office with the statement that "the Shanghai Indoor Environment Purification Association is willing to do auxiliary work, assist the construction committee in the clean indoor environmental assessment of the plant, clean engineering enterprise practitioners training and other technical issues", emphasizing the association's ability and auxiliary role in solving the technical problems of "clean qualification". It laid a good foundation for the association's industry pilot of the issuance of the "clean qualification" to industry professionals, the Shanghai Construction Industry Management Office's willingness to delegate authority to the association to execute administrative licenses, to assess and issue the "Shanghai Air Purification Engineering Professional Contracting Enterprise Qualification".

However, the Shanghai Construction Industry Administration Office adopted strategies such as "avoidance", and "co-opt or control" in response to the strategic actions of the Shanghai Association. To avoid the workload and policy risks caused by the introduction of new policies, the Shanghai Municipal Construction Industry Administration Office adopted an "evasive" strategy in response to the association's policy advocacy. It rejected the policy through inaction. Once the instructions of the Shanghai Mayor Han Zheng were received, then the Shanghai Construction Industry Management Office started the policy formulation and implementation of the "clean qualification certification". As it happened, the Shanghai Association was willing to contribute and had the corresponding technical capabilities. The Shanghai Construction Industry Management Office, unable to refuse in any case, was able to make use of the association staff to implement the "clean qualification certification" through the method of "adoption". At first, as may be expected, the Shanghai Construction Industry Management Office did not fully trust the technical capabilities of the association, and asked the association to pilot the industry. The results of the pilot project over four years allowed the Shanghai Construction Industry Management Office to follow the "influence and control" of the association, so much so that it even "codified" it as an agency to perform government functions.

3.2.5 Changes in Government Behavior Influenced by the Association

First, the policy advocacy of the Shanghai Association changed the inaction of the Shanghai Construction Industry Administration Office, allowing it to introduce the "Shanghai Air Purification Engineering Professional Contracting Enterprise Qualification Certification" policy. As early as 2006, the Shanghai Association advocated for the policy to the Shanghai Municipal Government and relevant functional departments through various channels. It argued that the policy should be implemented as soon as possible, so as to better meet the huge demand of Shanghai's indoor environment cleaning market and safeguard the interests of Shanghai local air purification engineering companies.

It was not until 2008, through Song Yiqiao, then vice chairman of the Shanghai Municipal Committee of the CPPCC, that the association sent the letter to Han Zheng, then mayor of Shanghai, who issued instructions to the Shanghai Construction Industry Management Office. Inaction in the department transformed into initiating contact with the Shanghai Association to discuss formulating the "Shanghai Air Purification Engineering Professional Contracting Enterprise Qualification Certification" policy.

Second, the Shanghai Association pushed for the "Shanghai Air Purification Engineering Professional Contracting Enterprise Qualification Certification" pilot program. The success of that venture enhanced the trust of the Shanghai Construction Industry Management Office in the association's business capabilities. This led to the transfer and decentralization of the government's "clean qualification certification" administrative licensing power. Many industry associations conduct industry training and transmit information on behalf of the government. Few actually conduct the government's licensing functions. Even the trade associations that have the administrative licensing power to enforce administrative regulations are mostly former government departments that were converted. The Shanghai Association had no history of administrative dependency and only represented the interests of its members.

In 2010, Shanghai government experienced the "building collapse incident" during the two sessions. This hindered the introduction of the Shanghai Municipal Construction Commission's "clean qualification certification" policy. The Shanghai Association maintained its advocacy posture. It took the initiative to pilot the "Shanghai Air Purification Engineering Professional Contracting Enterprise Capacity Assessment" in the industry. Although this enterprise capability assessment was not as authoritative as the government-issued qualification certification, it proved an important step for the implementation of the policy. In 2014, after nearly 4 years of pilot work, the association's business ability in "clean qualification certification" won the trust of the Shanghai Construction Industry Management Office, and finally obtained the consent to directly issue the "Shanghai Air Purification Engineering Professional Contracting Enterprise Qualification" license on behalf of the Shanghai Municipal Housing and Construction Commission according to the assessment results of the "Shanghai Air Purification Engineering Professional Contracting Enterprise Capacity Assessment".

In short, the policy participation action of the Shanghai Association was successful.

First, the association's policy participation actions successfully grappled with a complex and changing external environment. The lack of policies and regulations of the Ministry of Housing and Urban-Rural Development enabled the Shanghai Association to advocate for a local policy. The changes in the environment for policy implementation during the two sessions allowed the association to take the initiative. These efforts resulted in the "Shanghai Air Purification Engineering Professional Contracting Enterprise Qualification Certification" industry pilot and the promulgation of Document No. 19 [2011] by the General Office of CPC Shanghai Municipal Committee "Guiding Opinions on Further Strengthening the Construction of Social Organizations in the City", which provides policy support for the association to execute administrative licenses as agents.

Second, the Shanghai Association fully mobilized multi-channel resources such as member enterprises, social resources, and scientific and technological business to carry out policy participation actions. The association used Secretary-General Wang Fang's status as a member of the CPPCC, the proposal of the mayors' meeting, the direct advocacy of Song Yiqiao, then vice chairman of the Shanghai Municipal Committee of the CPPCC, to the mayor of Shanghai, and the use of conference room symposiums, on-site discussions, and discussions for government counselors during the policy demonstration period to achieve policy participation actions.

Finally, the Shanghai Association carried out fruitful strategic interaction with the Shanghai Municipal Government and relevant functional departments. Faced with the evasive strategy of the Shanghai Municipal Construction Industry Management Office, the association obtained the instructions of Han Zheng, then mayor of Shanghai, through the letter "Shanghai Indoor Environment Purification Association in Solving the Difficulties Encountered by the Qualification of Enterprise Air Purification Engineering Professional Contracting Enterprises". Mayor Zheng's orders forced the Shanghai Municipal Construction Industry Management Office to launch the "Shanghai Air Purification Engineering Professional Contracting Enterprise Qualification Certification". After affirming the association's business capabilities, the government allowed the association to be its agent and perform the administrative function of "clean qualification certification", which was the ultimate goal of the association's policy participation.

4 The Zhejiang Bicycle and Electric Vehicle Industry Association Strives for the "Right to Speak"

With the concepts of low-carbon travel, environmental protection, and comfort deeply rooted in daily life, the public's demand for convenient, labor-saving, economical, and environmentally friendly electric bicycles continues to increase. In the second half of 1998, Zhejiang Province took the lead in the country in including electric bicycles in the category of non-motor vehicle management. Electric bicycles were legally produced, operated, and put on the road by this benign development track. The annual growth rate of the bicycle and electric vehicle industry in Zhejiang Province increased year after year, creating many influential national electrical bicycle brands, such as Lvyuan, Philip, Qunfang, Wolong, Xinfu, Hengguang, Benbao, Xiaofei, Harriston, Moraque, Jinlu, and Lanbei, among others. Zhejiang Province is one of the largest electric bicycle production bases in China. Production is mainly concentrated in Taizhou, Hangzhou, Ningbo, Jinhua, Jiaxing, Shaoxing, and other places.

The Zhejiang Bicycle and Electric Vehicle Industry Association (hereafter Zhejiang Association) was established in August 1993, which was transformed from the state-owned enterprises of that year. As of the time of this study, there were nearly 300 member companies, most of which were engaged in the production of bicycles and electric bicycles, parts, accessories, and batteries. The association's organizational structure included its general assembly, council, and secretariat. The secretariat consisted of the office, information center, exhibition work department, and finance department. In 2012, the annual income of the association was about 2 million yuan, of which about 30% came from membership fees, and the other 70% came from the service income generated by the association's exhibitions. Annual expenditures were basically the same as annual income, of which salary expenditures accounted for 50%, office expenditures were between 20 and 30%, and the associations magazines such as "Zhejiang Bicycle" consumed about 10% of the annual budget. In 2014, the association had 11 full-time staff, 8 of whom had college degrees or above. Zhang Shunrong, then chairman of the association, and Chen Jianlong, then executive vice chairman and secretary-general, were leaders of the first enterprises in the industry before the transformation of the association. The association hosts the "China Zhejiang International Bicycle and Electric Vehicle Exhibition" every year, and has been rated as an excellent exhibition project by the Hangzhou Municipal Government and the West Lake Expo for many years. In addition, the association promotes bicycle culture, actively advocates and organizes bicycle riding activities, and promotes "green transportation" and the development of bicycle industry.

4.1 The Road to Policy Participation

While the number of electric bicycle traffic accidents continued to rise sharply, the traffic safety management of electric bicycles was underdeveloped. There have always been problems with the management of traffic behavior, collecting evidence for excessive speeding, and investigating and dealing with illegal acts on the road. To further strengthen the management and standardization of the traffic behavior of electric bicycles, the central and local government law enforcement departments tried to standardize the production standards of electric bicycle manufacturers. It was thought that it would help if there was increased supervision of source links such as the production and sales of electric bicycles. However, the government's new standards greatly increased the cost of electric bicycle manufacturers. This in turn lead to the closure of a large number of electric bicycle manufacturers. As these unintended consequences played out, the Zhejiang Association began policy participation activities such as "influencing and revising the 'Hangzhou Electric Bicycle Management Regulations and Policy Content'", "calling on the National Standardization Administration to suspend the implementation of 'electric motorcycles, standards'", and "speaking on the management of electric bicycles at the public hearing of the Zhejiang Provincial People's Congress".

4.1.1 The Association Affects Policy Through the "Hangzhou Electric Bicycle Management Regulations"

From 2006 to 2008, the number of electric bicycle traffic accidents in Hangzhou rose significantly. Only in 2008, 875 road traffic accidents involved electric bicycles in the city of Hangzhou, Zhejiang Province. They resulted in 973 injuries. There were 141 fatal accidents involving electric vehicles, resulting in 152 deaths, accounting for 17.63 of the total number of traffic fatalities, an increase of 44 or 40.75% compared to

2007, accounting for 48.41% of traffic fatalities involving non-motor vehicles.[2] The Hangzhou Municipal Government planned to issue, in 2009, "Regulations on the Administration of Electric Bicycles in Hangzhou" and formulated an implementation plan to strengthen the management of electric bicycles.

In early March 2009, the Zhejiang Association heard that the Hangzhou Municipal Government was going to formulate its regulations and implementation plan for the management of electric bicycles. It immediately convened member enterprises to hold a small seminar to discuss the proposed "Hangzhou Electric Bicycle Management Regulations" and to gather opinions so it might protect the members' interests. At the seminar, various manufacturers put forward their opinions about some of the provisions in the regulations. The meeting resulted in the formation of two core opinions.

First, the association considered inappropriate this clause from the proposed regulation—"the mass (weight) of the electric bicycle is not greater than 40kg"—for three reasons. First, that national standard was drafted and formulated in 1999, when electric bicycles were first introduced. Some of the provisions were no longer suitable for the development of the electric bicycle industry today. The National Bicycle Standards Committee proposed to revise the national standard in 2004. A draft submitted to the National Standardization Administration raised the maximum vehicle weight of the original standard. Second, due to the release of the national standard in 2005, the Zhejiang Provincial Bureau of Technical Supervision adopted its local standard, "Zhejiang Electric Bicycle Safety Technical Requirements", which raised the vehicle quality standard to 50kg. After the standard was released, the 50kg standard was strictly implemented in the review of the Zhejiang Province license catalog. This provision was taken as a veto, which played an important role in standardizing the development of the electric bicycle industry. Third, the proportion of electric bicycles with weight below 40 kg was less than 5%. Only lithium battery electric vehicles and 24V student cars could meet the weight requirement. The lithium battery electric bicycles were expensive, based on immature technology, and unstable, making them unattractive to consumers. The driving time of the 24V electric

[2] "In 2008, 152 people died in traffic accidents with electric vehicles, the city will introduce relevant management regulations" Hangzhou.com.cn, January 19, 2009, http://www.hangzhou.com.cn/20090112/ca640947.htm.

vehicles was relatively short and was not suitable for the mass consumer market. The 36V vehicles using lead-acid batteries within the 40kg weight requirements were also not viable.

Second, to manage the scope of the regulations, the association believed that the Hangzhou municipal government should not investigate the electric bicycles produced by Hangzhou electric bicycle enterprises that do not meet the regulations. The products produced by Hangzhou electric bicycle enterprises were for the Hangzhou market, but they were also sold in the province, other parts of the country, and on the international market. Adopting a 40kg standard for electric bicycles across the board was not necessary. The introduction of such a policy would be fatal to Hangzhou's electric bicycle enterprises. It would also be unfair to Hangzhou's electric bicycle manufacturers. Many would close and thousands of employees would lose their jobs, causing social unrest.

On March 12, 2009, after confirming the above two opinions, the Zhejiang Association submitted the "Opinions on the Administrative Regulations of Hangzhou Electric Bicycles" to the Hangzhou Municipal Government for its decision-making reference. The Hangzhou Municipal Government and relevant functional departments, such as the Hangzhou Municipal Public Security Bureau, the Administration for Industry and Commerce, and the Quality and Technical Supervision Bureau, attached great importance to the Zhejiang Association's submission. It sent a special research team to Hangzhou electric bicycle manufacturers and associations representing the voice of the industry to conduct research and to verify the above problems.

On March 23, 2009, on the basis of preliminary research, the Hangzhou Municipal Public Security Bureau, Administration for Industry and Commerce and Quality and Technical Supervision Bureau jointly issued the "Notice on Strengthening the Registration Management of Electric Bicycles Production and Sales". The notice stipulates that the main technical performance indicators and marking of electric bicycles listed in the "Hangzhou Electric Bicycle Production and Sales Registration Catalog" (hereinafter referred to as the "Catalog") must meet nine requirements. These standards would deal a huge blow to electric bicycle manufacturers in Zhejiang Province. If the requirements of the Regulations were strictly followed, manufacturers would have to explore new markets outside Hangzhou, dealers would return e-bikes that did not meet the standards, and people would not buy e-bikes because of the high cost of licensing. In addition, many electric vehicle manufacturers were confused by the electric vehicle standards. Quan Shuiming, general manager of Zhejiang Lanbei Automobile Industry Co., Ltd., commented that "electric vehicles have national standards, there are Zhejiang provincial standards, and now the city has introduced 'another standard'". "Whether the whole vehicle is qualified is based on the 'provincial standard', but the license plate will be based on the 'municipal standard', and the cost of enterprise operation will then rise sharply".[3]

On April 12, 2009, in order to reduce losses and win the "right to speak", the Zhejiang Association convened an internal meeting of the heads of more than 20 electric vehicle enterprises to discuss countermeasures. After the meeting, the Zhejiang Association contacted the Hangzhou quality inspection department. After discussing the implementation of the Catalogue, the two parties reached an agreement: If the vehicles produced do not meet the municipal standard but meet the national standard, they can continue to be produced, but they must be sold outside the city. If they are to be sold in Hangzhou, they must meet the city standard.

On June 10, 2009, the General Office of Hangzhou Municipal People's Government issued Document No. 211 [2009] "Implementation Plan for Strengthening the Management of Electric Bicycles Catalog", which stipulates that "public security, quality supervision, industry and commerce and other departments will organize joint actions to strictly follow the requirements of the Notice on Strengthening the Registration and Management of the Production and Sales of Electric Bicycles, and increase the supervision and management of the production, sales, licensing, use and other links of electric bicycles. Implement a joint reporting system of three departments".

So far, Zhejiang Association had achieved a certain victory in the game with the Hangzhou Municipal Government on the management regulations of electric bicycles. The "Hangzhou Electric Bicycle Production and Sales Registration Catalogue", issued by the Hangzhou Municipal Government, adopted the association's policy recommendation plan, stipulating that "the mass (weight) of the whole vehicle is not more than 50kg". On the matter of whether the maximum speed should be

[3] Wang Wenzheng, Hangzhou, controversial electric bicycle restrictions, June 05, 2009, Zheshang Magazine, http://finance.sina.com.cn/china/dfij/20090605/10046309442.shtml.

greater than 20km/h, however, the association believed it had not been successful.

4.1.2 The Association Calls on the National Standardization Administration to Suspend the Implementation of the "Electric Motorcycle" Standard

In early December 2009, the Standardization Administration of the People's Republic of China issued four relevant standards, including "Safety Requirements for Electric Motorcycles and Electric Mopeds", "Test Methods for Dynamic Performance of Electric Motorcycles and Electric Mopeds", "Test Methods for Energy Consumption Rate and Driving Range of Electric Motorcycles and Electric Mopeds", and "General Technical Conditions for Electric Motorcycles and Electric Mopeds". They were scheduled to be officially implemented on January 1, 2010. It was stipulated that "electric bicycles of more than 40 kilograms and a speed of more than 20 kilometers per hour are called mopeds or electric motorcycles, which are classified as motor vehicles". If this national standard were implemented, then driving such a vehicle would mean getting a driver's license, licensing the vehicle as an automobile, and buying insurance.

These several government documents seriously damaged the interests of member enterprises. At the time, there were more than 200 electric vehicle manufacturers in Zhejiang Province, but less than 10 enterprises with motorcycle production qualifications. Given the technical conditions at that time, requiring the production of "electric bicycles under 40 kilograms and below 20 kilometers per hour" was equivalent to abandoning the market. "If this new standard is followed, Zhejiang electric vehicle companies will face the danger of withdrawing from the industry as a whole". Chen Jianlong, vice president and secretary-general of Zhejiang Association, said frankly.[4] To this end, the Zhejiang Association convened the Zhejiang Electric Bicycle Vehicle and Parts Manufacturers to discuss how to affect the implementation of the new "electric motorcycle" standard.

On December 6, 2009, in the face of opposition from various provinces and cities, the National Standardization Administration

[4] New electric motorcycle standards lead to industry "backlash" Zhejiang electric car companies put words to quit, Zhejiang Daily, December 9, 2009.

provided on its official website its "Explanation on the relevant situation of electric motorcycle standards", stating that "electric bicycles and electric mopeds are two products with obviously different characteristics", and that "at present, electric bicycles purchased and used by consumers that meet the standards are non-motor vehicles, and the owner does not need to obtain a driver's license and a motor vehicle license plate". For electric bicycles that do not meet the standards, it is not clearly stated whether they belong to motor vehicles or non-motor vehicles.

On December 8–10, 2009, the Zhejiang Association found that the National Standardization Administration had no intention of suspending the implementation of its electric motorcycle standard and decided to appeal to various media. They pushed the narrative that the electric motorcycle standard issued by the National Standardization Administration could not be connected with the standards implemented in many cities in Zhejiang Province, which would directly cause the overall electric vehicle industry in Zhejiang Province to withdraw from the market. On December 8, 2009, the Zhejiang Daily published "Zhejiang Electric Vehicles 'Very Hurt'". On December 9, 2009, Zhejiang Online News Website published "New standard for electric motorcycles leads the industry to rebound, Zhejiang electric vehicle companies have withdrawn", and so on.

On December 11, 2009, the National Standardization Administration once again issued an article entitled "Experts answer on electric motorcycle and electric bicycle standards" on its official website, saying that "electric motorcycles are a kind of motorcycle". As motorcycles have historically been managed as motor vehicles, the commission invoked electric bicycle standards reiterating that "the maximum speed of electric bicycles should not be greater than 20km/h, and the weight of the whole vehicle should not be greater than 40kg". However, those electric bicycles that exceeded those standards, which the public was most concerned about, were still not mentioned in the article.

In this regard, Zhejiang Association believed that in addition to representing the interests and needs of the electric vehicle industry in Zhejiang Province, it was also necessary to contact the China Bicycle Association and other provincial and municipal bicycle industry associations in the electric bicycle production base. These included the Shanghai Bicycle Industry Association, the Tianjin Bicycle Industry Association, the Hangzhou Electric Vehicle Chamber of Commerce, the Shandong

Bicycle Association, etc. The Zhejiang Association sought to communicate and discuss a joint letter to the relevant departments of the central government, requesting the revision of the standard policy documents of the National Standardization Administration. They also discussed the possibility of a public appeal to "Suspend the implementation of electric motorcycle standards", for otherwise Chinese electric bicycle market would be significantly impacted.

On 15 December 2009, the Zhejiang Association issued an "appeal" on the websites of the China Bicycle Association with the Tianjin Bicycle Association and Shanghai Bicycle Association to suspend the implementation of electric motorcycle standards. The Zhejiang Association's statement was an "urgent call for suspension of the implementation of electric motorcycle standards and revision of electric bicycle standards as soon as possible". It went on to state that the four national standards (hereinafter referred to as "electric motorcycle standards") officially issued by the National Standardization Administration such as the "Safety Requirements for Electric Motorcycles and Electric Mopeds" (GB24155-2009) and the "General Technical Conditions for Electric Motorcycles and Electric Mopeds" (GB/T24158-2009) were not scientific, reasonable, realistic, or representative. The appeal urged that that the implementation of the electric motorcycle standards be suspended. The new national standards for electric bicycles should be revised to make reasonable adjustments to the main technical indicators of the original national standard, to set the maximum speed of electric bicycles within a reasonable range of 26 and 30 km/h, and to adjust the weight of electric bicycles to no more than 40 kg (excluding battery packs).

On the afternoon of December 16, 2009, the National Standardization Administration issued the notice of Document No. 98 [2009] suspending the implementation of the four national standards, including the "General Technical Conditions for Electric Motorcycles and Electric Mopeds", and at the same time accelerating the revision of the national standard of "General Technical Conditions for Electric Bicycles" (GB17761-1999).

4.1.3 The Association Spoke at the Public Hearing of the Zhejiang Provincial People's Congress on the Topic of "Electric Bicycle Management"

On September 6, 2010, the Standing Committee of the Zhejiang Provincial People's Congress held its first public hearing on road safety law enforcement inspections, with 16 speakers and 25 observers. There were four public hearings on motor vehicle driver management, electric bicycle management, investigation, and punishment of traffic violations, and the establishment and implementation of road traffic safety social assistance funds. Six of the 16 speakers made statements on the management of electric vehicles, speeding, and overweight vehicles, making the topic of "electric bicycle management" become an issue with the largest number of speakers and the most controversial content. This topic became a topic of debate at the public hearing for some time.

Chen Jianlong, then vice president and secretary-general of the Zhejiang Association, as a representative of the association, was invited to attend the public hearing and spoke. First, the lag of national standards seriously affected the healthy development of the industry and increased the difficulty of management. Due to the inconsistency of products, standards, requirements, and management, the implementation of catalogs in various places are not uniform. Even in Zhejiang Province, it is not uniform. For example, Wenzhou City does not allow electric bicycles to be licensed; Hangzhou City needs to re-declare the city's directory but lacks the authority from the province to do so. Second, the increase in traffic accidents involving electric bicycles cannot be blindly attributed to electric bicycles themselves. It is understood that a large part of these accidents involving electric bicycles are caused by car violations or cyclists riding not in accordance with traffic regulations. They are not caused by the excessive speed of the electric bicycles. Finally, he suggested that the Zhejiang Provincial People's Congress formulate management measures under the framework of relevant national laws and regulations. Every jurisdiction in the province should abide by the Zhejiang Province electric bicycle catalog so there will be unified licensing and unified management. This will improve the effectiveness, seriousness, and management of the catalog. Relevant government functional departments should strengthen the source management of electric bicycle enterprises as well as their supervision of the production and sales links.

From September to October 2012, the Zhejiang Association, as an important member, was invited many times to participate in the formulation and introduction of Zhejiang Electric Bicycle Management Measures.

4.2 *Case Analysis of Policy Participation*

4.2.1 External Environment for Policy Participation

The external environment for the Zhejiang Association's policy participation was as such: electric bicycle traffic accidents in Hangzhou continued to rise sharply; many problems still plagued the traffic safety management of electric bicycles; the social controversies arose due to the new standards for electric motorcycles; and, the problem of speeding and overweight electric vehicles in Zhejiang Province had become the focus of social attention. The above external environment prompted national, provincial, and municipal departments to make new regulations and adjustments to the production standards of electric vehicles. In that environment, the Zhejiang Association advocated for revising policies that were about to be, or had already been, introduced or are to be introduced. It conducted policy participation activities at different administrative levels of government. These included "influencing the revision of Hangzhou Electric Bicycle Management Regulations", "calling on the National Standardization Administration to suspend the implementation of electric motorcycle standards", and "speaking at the public hearing of the Zhejiang Provincial People's Congress on the management of electric bicycles".

4.2.2 Ability to Participate in Association Policies

The Zhejiang Association's ability to participate is mainly reflected in the strong member interest representative, its human resources, and its deft mobilization of other resources when opportunities presented themselves.

First, the Zhejiang Association represented the interests of its members. This included examining the policy content and actual implementation of the "Hangzhou Electric Bicycle Management Regulations", speaking at the Zhejiang Provincial Public Hearing, and publishing the Urgent Call for the Suspension of Implementation of Electric Motorcycle Standards. Before the Hangzhou Municipal Government issued the Hangzhou Electric Bicycle Management Regulations, the Zhejiang Association successively convened member companies to hold several internal seminars to discuss policy responses. After the release of the Hangzhou Electric Bicycle Production and Sales Registration Catalog, and to reduce losses and compete for a certain right to speak, the association once again convened more than 20 member enterprises to meet to discuss countermeasures, and negotiated with the Hangzhou quality inspection department in the name of the association to change the implementation of existing policies.

Second, in terms of human resource advantages, the chairman and executive vice chairman of the Zhejiang Association and other association leaders played an important role. Chairman Zhang Shunrong was the leader of the original industry company before the transformation of the association. Zhejiang Provincial Government and related functional departments and the Hangzhou Municipal Government and related functional departments had a good relationship and friendship with him. Executive Vice President and Secretary-General Chen Jianlong had expertise in the electric bicycle industry and its technology. He understood the needs of member enterprises and had close exchanges with member enterprises. These advantages allowed the Zhejiang Association to access government channels and advocate for the interests of member enterprises during its policy participation activities.

Finally, in terms of the association's resource mobilization capacity, the Zhejiang Association mobilized both its internal and external resources such as member enterprises, news media, and other industry associations, to jointly promote the suspension of the implementation of the National Standardization Committee's electric motorcycle standards. In December 2009, the National Standardization Administration issued four relevant standards on electric motorcycles and electric mopeds, including the General Technical Conditions for Electric Motorcycles and Electric Mopeds", stipulating that "Electric bicycles weighing more than 40 kilograms and with speed of more than 20 kilometers per hour, which are called mopeds or electric motorcycles, are classified as motor vehicles". The Zhejiang Association mobilized member companies to pressure the National Standardization Committee through various channels. It also appealed to various media, such as the Zhejiang Daily, the Zhejiang Online News Website, etc., to make the reports like that "manufacturers would not be able to comply with the electric motorcycle standards issued by the National Standardization Administration Committee", and "Zhejiang Province's electric vehicle industry will withdraw from the market as a whole". The association also mobilized external resources such as the China Bicycle Association, the Shanghai Bicycle Industry Association, the Tianjin Bicycle Industry Association, the Hangzhou Electric Vehicle Chamber of Commerce, the Shandong Bicycle Association, and other associations to jointly write to relevant central departments to request that the standard policy documents of the National Standardization Administration be revised. They also publicly called for the suspension of the implementation of the electric motorcycle standards.

4.2.3 Policy Will at Different Levels of Government

Although the policy participation activities of the Zhejiang Association were aimed at the same goal, they were targeted at different administrative levels of government. Different levels of government have shown different policy will to the policy participation of Zhejiang Association.

First, the Hangzhou Municipal Government and relevant functional departments adopted an open and accepting attitude toward the association's policy participation. Traffic safety problems caused by electric bicycle traffic accidents in Hangzhou caused the government to take action but avoid conflicts with relevant national policies and regulations. The Hangzhou Municipal Government issued the Hangzhou Electric Bicycle Production and Sales Registration Catalog on March 23, 2009. It proposed that the main technical performance indicators and labeling must meet nine requirements before they could be listed in the catalog for production, sales, and license registration. However, the nine provisions of the catalogue severely limited the Hangzhou electric bicycle manufacturers and sales market. If implemented, it would cause a serious decline in the Hangzhou electric bicycle industry. Under the initiative and coordination of the association, the Hangzhou quality inspection department balanced traffic safety, existing national policies and regulations, and the economic development of Hangzhou's electric bicycle industry to reach an agreement with the Zhejiang Association. If the vehicles produced do not meet the "municipal standard" but meet the "national standard", they could continue to be produced. Such non-conforming products could be sold elsewhere but not in Hangzhou unless they met the municipal standard.

Second, the Standing Committee of the Zhejiang Provincial People's Congress and the relevant functional departments of the provincial government actively invited the association to participate in the formulation of relevant policies and standards. The production and sales of electric bicycles were an important economic area of growth for Zhejiang Province. The production and sales of electric bicycles in Zhejiang Province were at the forefront of the country. Products were exported to the United States, Japan, Italy, Southeast Asia, the Middle East, and other countries and regions. Zhejiang, along with Tianjin, Guangdong, Jiangsu, and Shanghai were the five major industrial bases of bicycle production and export in China. For the sake of economic growth, the Zhejiang provincial government made every effort to promote and support the development of the electric vehicle industry. As a provincial industry association, the Zhejiang Association was more familiar with industry conditions, including product technology level and the standards of the electric bicycle industry in Zhejiang Province, than the relevant government departments. On September 6, 2010, the Standing Committee of the Zhejiang Provincial People's Congress held a public hearing on road safety law enforcement for the first time. The Zhejiang Association was invited to participate and put forward corresponding suggestions and opinions on the formulation of Zhejiang's Electric Bicycle Management Measures. The association had by then become an important contributor to those measures.

Finally, the National Standardization Committee ignored the policy participation of Zhejiang Association. In early December 2009, after the National Standardization Committee issued the new electric motorcycle standard, the Zhejiang Association alerted the media, joined with other industry associations, and urged government to suspend the implementation of the new electric motorcycle standard. The National Standardization Committee did not respond. The Zhejiang Association then shifted its strategy to the national associations, such as the China Bicycle Association to press the National Standardization Committee to suspend the implementation of the new electric motorcycle standard. This successful strategy may be related to the fact that the Zhejiang Association only represented the electric bicycle production and sales enterprises within the administrative division of Zhejiang Province. The local interests and voices of the provincial industry associations were not enough to influence the polices of national-level institutions and organizations.

4.2.4 Strategic Interactions Between the Association and Different Levels of Government

The Zhejiang Association carried out active and effective strategic interactions with government departments at all levels, mainly adopting strategies such as "compromise" (consultation and negotiation), "resistance" and "multi-organization cooperation". The core purpose of the policy participation of the Zhejiang Association was to rationalize the management methods and standard policies of electric bicycles.

In the process of policy participation, the Zhejiang Association adopted strategies such as "compromise" (consultation and negotiation), "resistance", and "multi-organization cooperation" in response to the responses and strategies of different governments. In the face of the Hangzhou Electric Bicycle Production and Sales Registration Catalog, the maximum speed was limited to no more than 20km/h and the mass (weight) of the whole vehicle to no more than 50kg. Because the catalog could not be modified or withdrawn, the association discussed these issues with the Hangzhou quality inspection department to negotiate the implementation of the catalog. It hoped that the requirements could be lowered during the catalog's implementation. After the National Standardization Administration introduced its electric motorcycle standard, the Zhejiang Association adopted a strategy of "resistance". With the help of news media, it bombarded the National Standardization Administration's electric motorcycle standard and stated that "Zhejiang's electric vehicle enterprises will withdraw from the market". After that, the association adopted a "multi-organizational cooperation" strategy, and Tianjin, Shanghai, and other bicycle associations each issued a "call" to suspend the implementation of electric motorcycle standards, and a joint petition to the National Standardization Committee.

In the face of the strategic actions of the Zhejiang Association, the Hangzhou Municipal Government adopted the strategy of "consultation and negotiation", the Standing Committee of the Zhejiang Provincial People's Congress and the provincial government adopted the strategy of "adoption", and the National Standardization Committee adopted the strategy of "avoidance". After consulting with the Zhejiang Association, the Hangzhou quality inspection department made a compromise, saying that if the vehicles produced do not meet the municipal standard but meet the national standard, they can continue to be produced. They may be sold in other places, but to be used in Hangzhou, they must meet the city's standards. This would not only ensure traffic safety, but also mean that the Catalog policy would not have to be withdrawn and there would be no conflict with national policy. This concession reduced the cost of electric vehicle manufacturers in Hangzhou. The Zhejiang Provincial People's Congress and the Zhejiang Provincial Government took up the co-option strategy, inviting the Zhejiang Association to speak at the public hearing and to participate in the drafting of the Zhejiang Province Electric Bicycle Management Measures. The National Standardization Committee avoided the association's bombardment of the electric motorcycle standard in the news media. And it also did not reply to the joint letter requesting suspension of the implementation of the new electric motorcycle.

4.2.5 Changes in Government Behavior Caused by the Association

First, the Zhejiang Association changed the strictness of the Hangzhou quality inspection department's implementation of the Hangzhou Electric Bicycle Production and Sales Registration Catalog. With the consent of the Hangzhou Municipal Government, the Hangzhou Municipal Public Security Bureau, the Bureau of Industry and Commerce, and the Quality Supervision Bureau decided to implement catalog management for electric bicycles produced, sold, and licensed in the administrative area of Hangzhou. Electric bicycle products had to comply with the General Technical Conditions for Electric Bicycles (GB17761-1999) of the People's Republic of China, and the main technical performance indicators and labeling of the products must meet nine requirements. This administrative change would have caused the electric vehicle production costs of electric vehicle manufacturers in Hangzhou to increase greatly and sales volume to fall precipitously. Naturally, this would have then triggered a strong protest from electric vehicle manufacturers in Hangzhou. In this regard, the Zhejiang Association repeatedly discussed and coordinated with the Hangzhou Municipal Quality Supervision Bureau. The Municipal Quality Supervision Bureau compromised in the specific implementation process. Products sold or used in the city must meet the city's standard. But products that meet the national standard may still be produced in the city.

Second, the policy participation of Zhejiang Association was an important force to prompt the National Standardization Committee to suspend the implementation of the new electric motorcycle standard. The relevant 4 standards for electric motorcycles and electric mopeds, including the General Technical Conditions for Electric Motorcycles and Electric

Mopeds issued by the National Standardization Committee, caused great repercussions in society. The Zhejiang Association used various channels such as media appeals and joint letters with relevant organizations to influence the policy implementation of the National Standardization Committee. Although the National Standardization Administration did not directly reply to the Zhejiang Association, it issued the Notice of Document No. 98 of the National Standardization Committee [2009], suspending the implementation of the four national standards, including the General Technical Conditions for Electric Motorcycles and Electric Mopeds. The Zhejiang Association was an important driving force for the National Standardization Administration to suspend the new electric motorcycle standard policy.

In short, the policy participation activities of Zhejiang Association were relatively effective, especially at the local level in Hangzhou. First, the Zhejiang Association fully mobilized internal and external resources such as member enterprises, other industry associations and chambers of commerce, and news media to carry out policy participation actions. Second, the Zhejiang Association and the Hangzhou Municipal Quality Supervision Bureau carried out effective strategic interaction, mutual consultation, and compromise. Ultimately, they changed the degree and the scope of a policy's implementation while maintaining the existing Catalog.

5 Multiple-Case Comparative Research and Analysis

The purpose of studying these four cases of policy participation by industry associations and chambers of commerce was to discover their common points and examine their common elements. The case study analysis was constructed as follows.

First, the external environment of the target association and industry used in the analysis framework was examined. The ability of the association or chambers of commerce to participate in policies was investigated. The dimensions of the government policy will that was displayed, and the strategic interactions employed by the association and the government were used to summarize the specific characteristics of the 14 different cases and events of these four industry associations and chambers of commerce. Second, the interaction mechanisms were analyzed as displayed between four industry associations and chambers of commerce and the government during the policy participation. Finally, the dynamic mechanism of mutual shaping between the external environment and strategic interaction was investigated.

5.1 External Environment, Dual Initiative, and Strategic Interaction

Based on the research dimensions of the external environment, the policy participation ability of industry associations and chambers of commerce, the government's policy will, and strategic interactions within the analysis framework are shown in Table 1. It lists the specific events of policy participation of the industry associations and chambers of commerce examined in the four cases, points out the specific content of each research dimension, and judges whether the policy participation results of each specific event were successful.

In the successful case events, the external environment was generally conducive to the policy participation of the industry association.[5] The government's policy will was basically the support, or active delegation of authority by, the government or relevant department. Each association's policy participation ability was manifested through human resources and resource mobilization. Strategic interaction was mostly manifested as "acquiescence or compliance" and "cooption or control" as well as "multi-organization cooperation" and other strategies. But there are also many successful cases of policy participation that do not show obvious interaction strategies. Successful case events were found in different types of policy participation. These include the policy advocacy by the Shanghai Association that led to the establishment of the Shanghai Air Purification Engineering Professional Contracting Enterprise Qualification Certification. A typical case of successful participation in decision-making was the Wenzhou Municipal Bureau of Commerce entrusting the Wenzhou Association to formulate the 1 + x series of policies for the development of Wenzhou e-commerce. A typical case of successful policy implementation was the administrative license of the Shanghai Association, which issued the Shanghai Air Purification Engineering Professional Contracting Enterprise Qualification. A typical case of the success of Private Benefit Government was the pilot of the Shanghai Air Purification Engineering

[5] The relationship between the external environment and strategic interactions will be further detailed later.

Table 1 Policy events, research dimensions, policy engagement outcomes, and types

The name of the industry association and chamber of commerce	*Specific incidents*	*External Environment*	*Ability to engage in policy*	*Government policy will*	*Strategic interactions*	*Policy engagement results*	*Type of policy involvement*
Taishun Small Hydropower Industry Association	Supervise and urge the county power bureau to implement the electricity price policy	Document No. 59 [1994] & Document No. 295 [1996] of Zhejiang Provincial Price Bureau	Executive Vice President He Xuchang	Supported by the Provincial Price Bureau		succeed	Supervise the effective implementation of policies
	Affect feed-in tariff adjustments	There is an oversupply of electricity	Executive Vice President He Xuchang	Supported by the Provincial Planning and Economic Commission		succeed	Policy advocacy

(continued)

Table 1 (continued)

The name of the industry association and chamber of commerce	*Specific incidents*	*External Environment*	*Ability to engage in policy*	*Government policy will*	*Strategic interactions*	*Policy engagement results*	*Type of policy involvement*
	The petition requests fair enforcement of Internet prices	Discriminatory pricing for institutional reasons	Executive Vice President He Xuchang mobilized 105 small hydropower owners	The municipality ignored it; the provincial party committee and the provincial government do not pay attention; Zhang Dejiang, secretary of the provincial party committee, instructed	Rebel and avoid compromise	Not entirely successful	Influencing the content of policy implementation

The name of the industry association and chamber of commerce	*Specific incidents*	*External Environment*	*Ability to engage in policy*	*Government policy will*	*Strategic interactions*	*Policy engagement results*	*Type of policy involvement*
	Cooperate with other associations to carry out electricity price policy negotiation games	Document [2006] 661 jointly issued by eight ministries	Executive Vice President He Xuchang mobilized the capacity of other small hydropower associations	Support from government functional departments such as the Provincial Price Bureau's Wage Department, the Provincial Water Conservancy Department's Hydropower Center, and other government functional departments	Multi-organization cooperation	succeed	Policy advocacy

(continued)

Table 1 (continued)

The name of the industry association and chamber of commerce	*Specific incidents*	*External Environment*	*Ability to engage in policy*	*Government policy will*	*Strategic interactions*	*Policy engagement results*	*Type of policy involvement*
E-commerce industry in Wenzhou	Submit policy proposals to the Wenzhou CPPCC meeting	Wenzhou's traditional industries urgently need to be transformed and upgraded	Chen Qixian, vice president of the association, is the director of the research committee of the Wenzhou Municipal Committee of Minjian	The secretary of the Wenzhou municipal party committee and the mayor of Wenzhou both ordered to accelerate the implementation of the proposal		succeed	Policy advocacy
	Formulate "'1 + X' series of policies for the development of e-commerce in Wenzhou"	Wenzhou's traditional industries urgently need to be transformed and upgraded	The association integrates the resources of enterprises, research institutions, financial institutions, and the media	The Wenzhou Municipal Bureau of Commerce authorized the association to formulate a series of policies	"Acquiescence or Compliance" vs. "Co-option or Control"	succeed	Participate in decision-making

The name of the industry association and chamber of commerce	*Specific incidents*	*External Environment*	*Ability to engage in policy*	*Government policy will*	*Strategic interactions*	*Policy engagement results*	*Type of policy involvement*
	Implement e-commerce in Wenzhou "1234" Engineering Policy	Wenzhou's traditional industries urgently need to be transformed and upgraded	The association combines resources such as capital flow, information flow, logistics, and business flow	Wenzhou Municipal Bureau of Commerce authorized to support the association to build "Wenzhou Financial E-commerce Public Service Platform"	"Acquiescence or Compliance" vs. "Co-option or Control"	succeed	Enforce policies
The name of the industry association and chamber of commerce	*Specific incidents*	*External environment*	*Ability to engage in policy*	*Government policy will*	*Policies mutually*	*Policy engagement results*	*Type of policy involvement*
Shanghai Indoor Environment Purification Industry Association	Advocate the establishment of "Shanghai Air Purification Engineering Professional Contracting Enterprise Qualification Certification"	lack of policies and regulations of the Ministry of Construction; Shanghai's demand for professional construction enterprises in purification engineering	Representativeness and autonomy of associations; the association mobilizes members and external resources	Instructions from Shanghai Mayor Han Zheng		Succeed	Policy advocacy

(continued)

Table 1 (continued)

The name of the industry association and chamber of commerce	*Specific incidents*	*External environment*	*Ability to engage in policy*	*Government policy will*	*Policies mutually*	*Policy engagement results*	*Type of policy involvement*
	Carry out the demonstration and investigation of "Shanghai Air Purification Engineering Professional Contracting Enterprise Qualification"	Purification engineering professional construction enterprises strongly demand	Mobilization of enterprises, officials, etc		Multi-organization cooperation		Participate in decision-making
	Pilot "Shanghai Air Purification Engineering Professional Contracting Enterprise Capacity Assessment" in the industry	Changes in the implementation of the policies of the Construction Committee during the two sessions	Representation and autonomy of associations	The Shanghai Municipal Construction Industry Administration Office agreed in principle		Succeed	Private government

The name of the industry association and chamber of commerce	*Specific incidents*	*External environment*	*Ability to engage in policy*	*Government policy will*	*Policies mutually*	*Policy engagement results*	*Type of policy involvement*
	On behalf of the administrative license, the "Shanghai Air Purification Engineering Professional Contracting Enterprise Qualification" is assessed and issued	General office of CPC Shanghai Municipal Committee issued the Document No. 19 [2011]	Human resources, financial resources	The Shanghai Municipal Construction Industry Administration Office decentralizes and transfers functions	"Acquiescence or Compliance" vs. "Co-option or Control"	Succeed	Policy enforcement

(continued)

Table 1 (continued)

The name of the industry association and chamber of commerce	*Specific incidents*	*External environment*	*Ability to engage in policy*	*Government policy will*	*Policies mutually*	*Policy engagement results*	*Type of policy involvement*
Zhejiang Bicycle and Electric Vehicle Industry Association	Affect the policy content of the "Hangzhou Electric Bicycle Management Regulations"	Electric bicycle traffic accidents in Hangzhou continue to rise sharply, and there are many problems in the management of electric bicycle traffic safety	Human resources; mobilize and convene member companies to discuss and formulate countermeasures and suggestions	The Hangzhou Municipal Public Security Bureau, Hangzhou Municipal Administration for Industry and Commerce and the Quality and Technical Supervision Bureau listened to the opinions of the association	Resistance and compromise	Not entirely successful	Influence the content and implementation of government policies

The name of the industry association and chamber of commerce	*Specific incidents*	*External environment*	*Ability to engage in policy*	*Government policy will*	*Policies mutually*	*Policy engagement results*	*Type of policy involvement*
	Call on the National Standardization Administration to suspend implementation standard	The new standard of "electric motorcycle" has caused social controversy	Human resources; mobilize resources such as the media, other industry organizations, etc		Multi-organization and National Standardization Administration avoidance	Succeed	Suspension of implementation of the impact policy
	Participated in the public hearing of the Zhejiang Provincial People's Congress and appealed	The problem of over speeding and overweight electric vehicles in Zhejiang Province has become the focus of social attention	Chen Jianlong, vice president and secretary-general of the association, has the business knowledge and ability	Invited by the Legislative Affairs Office of the Standing Committee of the Zhejiang Provincial People's Congress			Policy advocacy

Professional Contracting Enterprise Capacity Assessment by the Shanghai Association. The common denominator of successful policy engagement in all of the above was that the local government adopted a supportive or empowering attitude toward the policy engagement of the associations.

In the case of incomplete success, the Taishun Small Hydropower Industry Association's petition for fair implementation of the online price policy was a typical case characterized by the above research dimensions. The discriminatory pricing problem caused by institutional reasons was the external environment. Executive Vice President He Xuchang was well versed in the rules of the official game and had rich management experience. The association's mobilization of 105 small hydropower owners to petition showed the "ability of the association to participate in policies". The municipal government council, the provincial party committee and the provincial government did not pay attention to it, and the provincial party secretary Zhang Dejiang's instructions were "government policy will". The association first adopted a strategy of resistance, to which the government responded with an evasion strategy. The interaction between the two became mutual compromise and a "strategic interaction". In the end, the association did not achieve a complete victory, but only changed part of the government's policy. Another specific event in which policy participation was not completely successful was the Zhejiang Association's effort to change the "Hangzhou Electric Bicycle Management Regulations". The external environment included electric bicycle traffic accidents in Hangzhou continued to rise sharply along with many other problems in the traffic safety management of electric bicycles. The association's human resources, mobilization, convening of member enterprises for discussion, formulation of countermeasures and suggestions, etc., revealed the "association's policy participation abilities". The Hangzhou Municipal Public Security Bureau, the Hangzhou Municipal Administration for Industry and Commerce, and the Quality and Technical Supervision Bureau only listened to the association's opinion, thereby revealing "the will of government policy". Resistance and compromise were "strategic interactions". Ultimately, the association did not achieve a complete victory, but only forced the relevant departments of the Hangzhou municipal government to adjust the way the policy was implemented. The two specific events in which the above-mentioned industry associations and chambers of commerce were not completely successful in policy participation had something in common: they belonged to the same "policy participation type", that is, they tried to influence and change the content of the policy implementation. Second, they all adopted the "strategic interaction" model of "resistance and compromise".

The comparison of specific events in multiple cases shows that the success of the policy participation of industry associations and chambers of commerce may occur in different types of policy participation. However, the support or authorization of the relevant local governments for that policy participation is the core element of success. If the external environment is good, it plays a role in promoting successful policy participation. In cases that policy participation was not completely successful, industry associations and chambers of commerce all adopted the "resist and compromise" strategy for specific events. Whether it is the policy participation of successful industry associations and chambers of commerce or the policy participation of incompletely successful industry associations and chambers of commerce, this reflects the dual initiative and two-way interactions between industry associations and chambers of commerce and governments.

5.2 *Changes in the External Environment*

Two-way strategic interactions between the government and industry associations and chambers of commerce were displayed in the four case studies. These experiences show that the government and industry associations and chambers of commerce carry out strategic interactions as the external environment changes. The following is a detailed discussion from two aspects: "the continuity and dynamics of the interaction between industry associations and chambers of commerce and the government" and "the mutual shaping of the external environment and strategic interaction".

5.2.1 *The Continuity and Dynamics of the Interaction Between Industry Associations and Chambers of Commerce and the Government*

In the context of policy participation, the interaction between industry associations and chambers of commerce and the government is by no means single, static, and fragmented. It is instead a continuous and dynamic evolutionary process around a certain policy issue. In this process, the government and industry associations and chambers of commerce adjust their own behaviors to achieve policy promotion and improvement.

The Taishun Small Hydropower Industry Association and Government Interaction Model

The participation of the Taishun Association in different small hydropower pricing policies lasted 10 years. Each stage showed the game and interaction, and even resistance and compromise, between the association and different government departments. In general, the policy participation of the Taishun Association effectively used existing policies and regulations, leaders' instructions, and cooperation with other organizations to interact with different levels of government, which can be summarized into two models.

In the first interaction model, the association rebels and the government avoids the compromise. This model was mainly reflected in the unreasonable formulation and unfair implementation of the small hydropower price policy that seriously damaged the interests of small hydropower owners. In response, the association carried out supervision and petitioning actions on behalf of the interests of small hydropower owners. Due to institutional reasons and pressure from interest groups, the relevant governments adopted an evasive attitude and acquiesced or allowed the introduction and continuation of the unfair electricity pricing policy. In the end, the relevant provincial departments and the provincial party secretary approved the mutual concessions and compromises between the association and the corresponding government departments. This mode of interaction has the characteristics of a long deadlock, with a large number of moves and countermoves, and both sides are not very satisfied with the results.

In the second interaction model, the association advocates, and the government support. Through the Provincial Planning and Economic Commission, the Taishan Association influenced the National Planning and Economic Commission to raise electricity prices. It also cooperated with other small hydropower industry associations to advocate new preferential policies and measures for electricity prices. Relevant government departments, such as the Provincial Planning and Economic Commission, the Provincial Price Bureau's Wage Department, the Provincial Water Conservancy Department, and the Hydropower Center also provided certain assistance and support. This mode of interaction was mainly based on the proactive advocacy and participation of industry associations and chambers of commerce that was then supplemented by the assistance and support of relevant governments. But the association was not satisfied with the results of the policy participation.

Wenzhou E-commerce Industry Association and Government Interaction Model

The time for the advocacy, formulation, and implementation of Wenzhou e-commerce policy by Wenzhou Association was relatively short. In less than half a year, the association began its policy advocacy, the official policy was announced, and the government then entrusted the association to implement some e-commerce policies. In general, the policy participation of the Wenzhou Association was effective as it interacted with the Wenzhou Municipal Government and its relevant functional departments. This can be summarized into the following interactive model of the Association advocates for a policy—the government accepts association's policy assistance—the association participates in the formulation of the policy—the government decentralizes power and association implements corresponding policies.

In the Wenzhou Association case, it initiated the policy advocacy with the "Opinions on Strengthening and Promoting the Development of E-commerce" in Wenzhou City through a proposal at the meeting of the Wenzhou Municipal Committee of the CPPCC. Because this policy met the government's needs for the economic transformation and development, the secretary of the Wenzhou Municipal Party Committee and the mayor both issued instructions to accelerate the policy's formulation and implementation. The Wenzhou Municipal Bureau of Commerce entrusted the Wenzhou E-commerce Industry Association to draft and formulate the "1 + X" series of policies to accelerate the development of e-commerce in Wenzhou. After officially promulgating the "Implementation Opinions on Accelerating the Development of E-commerce (Trial)" No. 137 of the Wen Zhengban [2012], the Wenzhou E-commerce Industry Association was also authorized to build the Wenzhou Financial E-commerce Public Service Platform and "Wenzhou Stainless Steel Industry Bulk Commodity E-commerce Public Service Platform". This model was mainly characterized by the government's initiative to delegate power, and the government's effective use, and ability to adopt the positive actions, of the association into policy formation. In this case, this was externally manifested in the form of cooperation between the government and the association. Both the association and the government were satisfied with the policy results because they each satisfied their interests in the policy's formulation and implementation.

Shanghai Indoor Environment Purification Industry Association and Government Interaction Model

The Shanghai Association's experience included 8 years before and after the "Shanghai Air Purification Engineering Professional Contracting Enterprise Qualification". It began with its initial advocacy and ended with the implementation of the administrative license. Each stage presents strategic interactions between the government and the association, which can be summarized in the following interactive model: The association advocates for the policy—the relevant government shirks and avoids—the association changes tactics and carries out research and demonstration discussions regarding the policy—the relevant government departments agrees that the association can pilot the implementation of the policy and then entrusts the association to implement the policy on behalf of the government.

The main process of this model was the association's dogged requests to the Shanghai Municipal Government and the Municipal Construction Commission to accelerate the establishment and implementation of the policy of "qualification certification of professional contracting enterprises for air purification projects" in Shanghai. At first, they were ignored and avoided. Two years later, through Song Yiqiao, president of the Shanghai Modern Service Industry Federation, the association successfully sent its letter "Shanghai Indoor Environment Purification Association in Solving the Difficulties Encountered by the Shanghai Indoor Environment Purification Association in Solving the Qualification Problems of Enterprise Air Purification Engineering Professional Contracting Enterprises" to the mayor of Shanghai. The mayor then sent instructions, which reversed the process of policy formulation and implementation. The Shanghai Municipal Construction Industry Administration Office required the association to produce a detailed report demonstrating the necessity and feasibility of establishing clean qualifications in Shanghai through investigation. The association was also allowed to pilot the new program. After 4 years of the pilot program, the association's "qualification certification" implementation ability was recognized by the Shanghai Municipal Construction Industry Management Office. It was then authorized to evaluate and issue the "Shanghai Air Purification Engineering Professional Contracting Enterprise Qualification" certificate on behalf of the Shanghai Municipal Construction Commission. This interaction mode was mainly characterized by the association's active policy participation, while the government was more passive. The interactions between the association and the government were also a process of mutual familiarity and trust and co-construction. For the government to proceed with an agency relationship, the association's ability to undertake government functions was examined by the relevant functional departments of the government in the form of a pilot operation.

Different from the cooperation model of the "Wenzhou E-commerce Industry Association and Government Strategic Interaction", in which the government actively entrusted and delegated power to the association, the cooperation mode of interaction between the Shanghai Association and the government was that the association sought out policies and powers from the government. The government appeared to be more passive and the process was relatively long. This is likely because the government had no endogenous need to formulate and implement the "Shanghai Air Purification Engineering Professional Contracting Enterprise Qualification", but rather took part passively in the project under pressure from the mayor's instructions.

Zhejiang Province Bicycle and Electric Vehicle Industry Association and the Government Interaction Mode

Zhejiang Association's policy preferences on electric bicycle production required different forms of policy participation at the level of Hangzhou City, Zhejiang Province, and the country as a whole. Each administrative level of government and its related functional departments had strategic interactions with the Zhejiang Association, which can be summarized in the following models.

First, it shows an interactive model of association resistance, government attention, and negotiation and compromise. This was mainly manifested in the association's expressed dissatisfaction with the nine provisions of the "Hangzhou Electric Bicycle Production and Sales Registration Catalog". The association in response convened more than 20 heads of electric vehicle enterprises to discuss countermeasures. They then jointly requested a change to the content of the nine provisions in the "Catalogue" during their dialogue with the Hangzhou Municipal Bureau of Quality and Technical Supervision. But these requests were rejected by the Hangzhou Municipal Quality Supervision Department because the "Catalogue" could not be withdrawn once published. It could only be slightly adjusted in the specific implementation matters. This mode of interaction was based on the active resistance of the industry association, supplemented by the compromise and cooperation of the relevant governments. Although the policy participation results were not satisfactory to the association, both sides made concessions.

The second model involves associations and media calling for boycotts, government evasion and disregard, associations joining other industry organizations in renewed calls for resistance, and National Standardization Committees compromising. This was reflected in the Zhejiang Association's call for the suspension of implementation of the new electric motorcycle standard issued by the National Standardization Committee, because it would have seriously damaged the interests of electric vehicle manufacturers. As for the appeals of the provincial industry associations, the National Standardization Administration, as a national-level institution, ignored them. Later, the Zhejiang Association, together with other provincial associations across the country and the China Bicycle Association, jointly issued an appeal to suspend the implementation of the new electric motorcycle standard. In the end, the National Standardization Committee [2009] No. 98 Circular suspended the implementation of the "New Electric Motorcycle Standard". This mode of interaction was still dominated by industry associations actively calling for resistance to existing policies and government departments adopting a passive and evasive attitude. The key to the success of the association's policy participation lies in working with other organizations to put pressure on the government to achieve changes in policy implementation.

The third model involved efforts in which the association advocates to become a policy adviser. This was reflected in the fact that representatives of the Zhejiang Association were invited to attend the public hearing of the Zhejiang Provincial People's Congress, and as an important member, the association was invited to participate in the discussion and consultation on the formulation and introduction of the management measures for electric bicycles in Zhejiang Province. This interaction mode was generally more benign. The government absorbed the association as a decision-making consultant to improve the scientific nature of the government's decision-making. By doing so, the association advocated for the policy interests of its members but as a decision-making consultant. This win–win relationship resulted in policy participation that was generally satisfactory to both parties.

5.2.2 *The Mutual Shaping of the External Environment and Strategic Interaction*

The interactions between industry associations and governments are a continuous and dynamic evolutionary process. In this process, the external environment may promote or regulate the interactions between the government and industry associations and chambers of commerce and the results of those interactions. At the same time, the interactions between industry associations and chambers of commerce and the government will also shape a new external environment which will in turn affect the strategic interactions of the parties involved.

The Mutual Shaping of the External Environment and the Interaction Between the Taishun Small Hydropower Industry Association and the Government

The interaction between the external environment and the Taishun Association and the government was shaped by the association's participation in the policy of different small hydropower prices over a 10-year period. In the policy participation, the Taishun Association and the government launched two different modes of interaction, which included "association resistance"/"government avoidance"/"mutual compromise" and "association advocacy"/"government support". The interaction between the associations and the government was influenced and shaped by the laws, regulations, policy documents of national and provincial government departments, and the important instructions of key provincial leaders. The interaction behavior of the government influenced the issuance and modification of policy documents of relevant departments of higher-level governments. In the course of the interaction between "the association resisting", "the government evading the other", and "compromising between the two sides", the association organized petitions to the Wenzhou municipal government and the Zhejiang provincial government. It opposed the unfair price for small hydropower set by the county and city governments. Governments at all levels tried to avoid engaging directly or gave these entreaties perfunctory treatment. Under this circumstance, the open letter submitted by the association to Zhang Dejiang, then secretary of the Provincial Party Committee, was approved and investigated in person. As the secretary of the provincial party committee, Zhang Dejiang's instructions and research broke the deadlock of the association and the government. The two sides negotiated and compromised. In the end, they presented the content of the compromise in the form of the policy text of the Document [2001] of Zhejiang Provincial Price Bureau "Notice on Matters Related to Local Public Small Hydropower On-grid Tariffs in Underdeveloped Areas". This was a strategic interaction that shaped a new external environment. In the process of the "Association Advocacy" and "Government Support" interaction, eight ministries and commissions, including the National Development and Reform Commission, the Ministry of Water Resources, and the Electricity Regulatory Commission, jointly issued Document No. 66 [2006] 1 "Notice on Accelerating the Structural Adjustment of the Electric Power Industry and Promoting the Healthy and Orderly Development of the Electric Power Industry". As part of the external environment, it promoted the effective policy advocacy of industry associations and chambers of commerce to relevant government departments and was supported by these government departments.

The Mutual Shaping of the External Environment and the Interaction Between Wenzhou E-Commerce Industry Association and the Government

Wenzhou E-commerce Industry Association advocates and participates in the formulation and implementation of e-commerce development policies in Wenzhou. In the process of this policy participation, the Wenzhou Association and the government launched the "Association Policy Advocacy"/"government entrusted policy formulation"/"association to participate in the formulation of policies"/"government decentralization"/"the association implements the corresponding policy". The above-mentioned interaction between the Wenzhou Association and Wenzhou Municipal Government was affected by the macro-external environment of Wenzhou's industry. This included the urgent need for traditional industries in Wenzhou to achieve transformation and upgrading through the cultivation and development of the e-commerce industry. These macro-external concerns ensured that the Wenzhou Association could advocate effectively because these industrial goals were known to be highly valued by the secretary of the Wenzhou Municipal Party Committee and the mayor. Further, the instructions of the secretary of the Wenzhou Municipal Party Committee and the mayor directly promoted the interaction and cooperation between the Wenzhou Municipal Bureau of Commerce and the association. After the Association participated in policy formulation, the Commerce Bureau continued to delegate part of the policy implementation power to the Association.

The Mutual Shaping of the External Environment and the Interaction Between Shanghai Indoor Environment Purification Industry Association and the Government

The Shanghai Association advocated for the establishment of an administrative licensure regime to implement the policy of the "Shanghai Air Purification Engineering Professional Contracting Enterprise Qualification". In this policy participation process, the Shanghai Association and the government launched an "Association policy advocacy"-"relevant government departments to prevaricate"-"Association again policy advocacy and research and demonstration"-"relevant government departments agreed in principle to the industry pilot"-"Association on behalf of the administrative license to implement the corresponding policy" interactive model. The interaction between the above-mentioned associations and the Government was influenced by a variety of external circumstances. Among them, the lack of policies and regulations of the Ministry of Construction as an external environment and the strong demand for professional construction enterprises in purification engineering in Shanghai caused the association to carry out policy advocacy for the government. However, the Shanghai municipal government department evaded engagement, making the interaction between the two unfulfilled. Song Yiqiao, president of the Shanghai Modern Service Industry Federation, changed the external environment by sending a letter to the then mayor of Shanghai, which resulted in instructions to the Shanghai Municipal Construction Management Office. The Shanghai Municipal Construction Management Office took the initiative to seek cooperation with the association to initiate the establishment and implementation of the policy of "Shanghai Air Purification Engineering Professional Contracting Enterprise Qualification". The General office of CPC Shanghai Municipal Committee issued Document No. 19 [2011] "The Guiding Opinions on Further Strengthening the Construction of Social Organizations in the City", which directly provided a basis and catalyst for the Shanghai Municipal Construction Management Office to authorize the association to implement the qualification recognition policy for the administrative license. This eventually led to the principal–agency relationship. At the same time, the strategic interaction between the association and the Shanghai Municipal Construction Management Office shaped a new cooperation mechanism and cooperation environment that resulted in "smooth cooperation channels between the association and the government".

The Mutual Shaping of External Environment and the Interaction Between Zhejiang Bicycle and Electric Vehicle Industry Association and the Government

The Zhejiang Association's advocacy for electric bicycle production standards was an on-the-ground policy participation at the municipal, provincial, and national levels. In the process, the Zhejiang Association launched three different interactive modes for different administrative levels of government. "Association resistance"-"Government attention"-"Discussion and compromise" interaction mode, "the association joint media calls for resistance"-"the government avoid ignoring"-"the association joint other industry organizations again calls for resistance"-"National Standardization Committee compromise" interaction mode, "Association advocacy"-"Association become a policy adviser" interaction mode.

The interactions between the above-mentioned associations and governments were affected by the external environment. These included "the public's discussion of the pros and cons of electric bicycles", "the existing policies restricting the standards of electric bicycles", "media public opinion rendering". At the same time, the interaction between the association and the government was also influenced as the existing policies, regulations, and public opinion changed. In the process of "Association resistance"/"Government attention"/"Discussion and compromise" Hangzhou electric bicycle traffic accidents jump sharply. This leads directly to the issuance of the Hangzhou Electric Bicycle Production and Sales Registration Catalog by the Hangzhou Municipal Government. That in turn changed in the interaction between the association and relevant departments of the Hangzhou Municipal Government. After convening an internal meeting of electric vehicle manufacturers, the association used that meeting to engage in dialogue with the Hangzhou quality supervision and inspection department. In the end, both sides made compromises and concessions.

In the process of "the association joint media calls for resistance"/"the government avoid ignoring/the association joint other industry organizations again calls for resistance"/"National Standardization Committee compromise", the external environment such as press and media and assistance from industry associations had an important impact on the interaction between the association and the National Standardization Administration. At first, the National Standardization Administration ignored the behavior of provincial industry associations. The Zhejiang

Association basically could not interact with the National Standardization Administration, while the joint appeals of other peer industry organizations and the publicity and opposition of the news media forced the National Standardization Administration to suspend the implementation of the newly introduced policies.

In the process of "Association advocacy"/"Association become a policy adviser", the Standing Committee of the Zhejiang Provincial People's Congress held a public hearing on road safety. This provided a good platform for the association to become a policy adviser to the Zhejiang provincial government and to thereafter formulate and introduce the management measures for electric bicycles.

The strategic interactions between the government and industry associations and chambers of commerce in the changing external environment are a two-way, continuous, and dynamic evolution process. The interactions between the government and industry associations and chambers of commerce are also promoted or influenced by the external environment. The government and the industry associations and chambers of commerce adjust their own behavior according to the external environment and the response of each other to achieve policy promotion and shape the external environment. In other words, the interactions between them are continuous, dynamic, and adaptable, while the external environment and strategic interaction are mutually shaped (see Table 2).

5.3 *Different Types of State–Society Relations in China*

Table 6.2 summarizes the different types of state–society relations in contemporary China as shown by the two-way strategic interaction between the government and industry associations and chambers of commerce in a changing external environment.

Case 1 illustrates that, to a certain extent, the policy participation of Chinese industry associations and chambers of commerce is "pluralistic". The association actively resisted the unfair implementation of relevant government policies to safeguard its members' interests, influenced the government through policy advocacy, and thereby realized the promotion and improvement of policies in the form of mutual compromise between industry associations and chambers of commerce and the government.

Case 2 shows that corporatism still exists in the relationship between the state and society in contemporary China. But it is different from the government control of previous years, for in "government domination"

Table 2 Strategic interaction between associations and governments, shaping of external environment and strategic interactions, and types of relations between the state and society

The name of the industry association and chamber of commerce	*Continuity and dynamism of interactions*	*The external environment and strategic interactions shape each other*	*Characteristics of the type of state–society relationship*
1. Taishun small hydropower industry	• The "association rebelled"/the government avoided"/ "compromise between the two sides" • "Association Advocates"/ "Government Assistance Support"	• National and provincial government policy documents/ instructions of the secretary of the provincial party committee and other external environmental influences on the interaction between the government and the association; • The compromise of government-association interaction has shaped the new external environment	Pluralism
2. Electronics industry in Wen	• "Association advocacy"/ "government entrusts policy formulation",/ "association drafts and formulates policies,"/ "government authorizes"/ "association implements policies"	• Industrial transformation and upgrading, the external environment promotes the policy advocacy of the association; • The secretary of the municipal party committee and the mayor issued instructions to promote interaction and cooperation between the government and the association	Government domination

(continued)

Table 2 (continued)

The name of the industry association and chamber of commerce	*Continuity and dynamism of interactions*	*The external environment and strategic interactions shape each other*	*Characteristics of the type of state–society relationship*
3. Shanghai indoor environment purification industry	• The "association" advocates"/"the government prevaricates and avoids the"/ "association research and demonstration",/ "the government agrees to pilot the"/"association in the industry to implement the policy on behalf of the administration"	• The external environment such as the lack of existing policies and regulations and the needs of enterprises promote the policy advocacy of the association; • The mayor's directive to reverse the way the association interacts with the government; • The documents of the general office of the municipal party committee promote the establishment of a principal–agent relationship between the government and the association; • Interaction between the government and associations shapes a new external environment for government–council cooperation	Corporatism

(continued)

Table 2 (continued)

The name of the industry association and chamber of commerce	*Continuity and dynamism of interactions*	*The external environment and strategic interactions shape each other*	*Characteristics of the type of state–society relationship*
4. Zhejiang Bicycle and Electric Vehicle Industry Association	• The "association resists"/the government attaches importance/ "discussing compromise" • The association called for rebellion,/the government avoided ignoring it,/the association and other industry organizations once again called for rebellion against the "one" national standard commission • "Association advocates"/ "association to become a policy adviser"	• The impact of the external environment such as public opinion and existing policies on the interaction between the government and the association; • The influence of the external environment such as the association of peer industry organizations and news media on the interaction behavior between the government and the association; • The interaction between the association and the government shapes the external environment such as existing policies, regulations, and public opinion	Syncretism

both the association and the government are more proactive, and the government continues to dominate associations by adopting them so that the two establish a symbiotic relationship of "dominance and control and default submission".

Case 3 shows that the "corporatist" character of the association's relationship with the government. The association actively advocated for favorable policy and sought cooperation with the government. As mutual trust increased, the association and the government formed an authorized, agent–principal relationship that included a communication channel for mutual consultation. The channel's survival was the convergence of the interests of the two.

Case 4 deviates from the existing theory of typical state–society relationship. This reveals the characteristics of the pluralistic changing relationship between the same association and different governments. Associations have the characteristics of pluralism such as resisting compromise and trying to change the implementation of policies to achieve members' interests as well as corporatist characteristics such as becoming policy advisers so as to become absorbed by the government. For that reason, they are not an existing type of state–society relationship, but it is referred to here as "blendism".

Although the above four cases show different types of interaction between industry associations and chambers of commerce and the government, they can all be interpreted under the framework of "two-way strategic interaction between industry associations and chambers of commerce and the government in the changing external environment". Whether it is pluralism, corporatism, or blendism, the strategic cooperation between the two sides is a common way to achieve sustainable interaction between the state and society in contemporary China. The four cases also show that this pluralism of state–society relations as it appears in the interactions between the state and society is not single, static, and rigid. It is instead pluralistic, dynamic, flexible, and adaptable. In addition, different types of state–society relations were exhibited between different industry associations and chambers of commerce and the government during the same period. The same industry association and chamber of commerce and different government departments also took on different roles and diverse relationships, which is a new trend in the evolution of state–society relations in contemporary China.

References

Wu X. Research on the development status and Countermeasures of Taishun small hydropower industry. China Water Power and Electrification, 2007, 7: 18-21.

Zhu K. Private capital and collective action of industry associations--A case study of small hydropower industry association in Taishun County, Wenzhou. Wenzhou Forum, 2007, 2: 8-21.

REFERENCES

CHAPTER 7

Conclusion and Discussion

Over the past 40 years of its reform and opening up, China's social organizations have achieved unprecedented development and prosperity from scratch. This has triggered sustained and heated discussions in academic circles on the relationship between the state and society. By the early 1990s, a large number of social organizations were represented by industry associations and chambers of commerce, breaking the pattern of high isomorphism between the state and society. Understandably, scholars were triggered to inquire into the budding of Chinese pluralism and began the hotly contested theoretical debates about Chinese pluralism and corporatism (Kennedy 2005; Unger and Chan 1996; White 1993; White et al. 1996; Yep 2000). By the end of the 1990s, many China scholars saw the relationship between social organizations and the government to be more inclined to the corporatist model (Hsu and Hasmath 2012; Unger 2008).

In the 2010s, researchers found that the relationship between social organizations and the government in China is neither pluralism nor complete corporatism, but a hybrid model of state control and social autonomy (Fan 2010; Teets 2013; Jing 2015). A growing number of scholars have observed the accelerating separation of the government and social organizations, the simultaneous strengthening of party building within social organizations, and the push to revitalize social organizations. These new trends highlight the further transformation of the

Y. Shen, *The Policy Participation of Business Associations in China*,
https://doi.org/10.1007/978-981-96-1096-9_7

state–society relationship, from the dual relationship between government and social organizations to the meta-relationship consisting of the party-government-social organization (Yu and Shen 2017).

Both diachronic research and the current facts show that the relationship between the state and society in contemporary China is not a single and static macrostructure, but a process of pluralism and dynamics. This book advocates for interpreting the pluralistic and dynamic relationship between the government and industry associations and chambers of commerce as the result of the "two-way strategic interaction between the government and industry associations and chambers of commerce in the changing external environment". This analytical framework emphasizes not only the strategic interactions between these two groups, but also emphasizes the mutual shaping of the external environment and their strategic interactions.

1 Research Findings

As this book shows, the relationship between China's industry associations and chambers of commerce and its government is both pluralistic and dynamic. This observation helps explain some of the aspects of the continuity and dynamics of the strategic interactions that lead to a mutual shaping of their strategic interactions and the external environment.

On the one hand, the strategic interaction between the government and industry associations and chambers of commerce is an evolutionary process. The government and the association, as dual agents, keeping an eye toward the changes in behavior of the other party and the external environment, adopt different strategies to adjust their own behavior based on their own interests and capabilities.

On the other hand, their strategic interactions and the external environment are mutually shaped. The external environment promotes or regulates the interaction mode and interaction results between the two groups, but the strategic interaction between industry associations and chambers of commerce and the government will also change the existing external environment. Among them, the external environment manifests as macro-policies, market demand, environmental differences in policy stages, and instructions from superior leaders. The dual initiative manifests through the stated objectives of government policies and the initiatives of industry associations and chambers of commerce. Strategic actions manifest as acquiescence, compromise, avoidance, resistance, manipulation, or cooperation.

Empirical results show that governments and industry associations and chambers of commerce take different strategic actions to achieve interaction goals based on their respective interests and capabilities. The changing external environment will affect the types, the pathways, and ultimately the results of these interactions. This study's analyses of large-sample data reveal that contemporary Chinese industry associations and chambers of commerce have diverse target objects, channels, and methods for policy participation. Nearly one-third of industry associations and chambers of commerce successfully influenced policy formulation or policy modification, and even stopped policy implementation through their interactions with the government. There is a significant effect on the way trade associations and chambers of commerce respond to government policy will through trade association and chamber of commerce policy participation.

When the case studies are compared, the interactions between industry associations and chambers of commerce and the government are revealed to be continuous, dynamic, and adaptable; the external environment and strategic interaction shape each other; and the "two-way strategic interaction between the government and industry associations and chambers of commerce in the changing external environment" displays the types of relations they engage in, which can toggle between pluralism, government domination, corporatism, and blendism.

This reflects the complexity of state–society relations in contemporary China. However, no matter the type of interaction, it can be interpreted under the framework of "two-way strategic interaction between industry associations and chambers of commerce and the government in the changing external environment". Strategic interaction and cooperation is an important way to achieve benign interaction between industry associations and chambers of commerce and the government. As always, the external environment plays a shaping role in their interactions.

2 Research Contributions

Unlike the existing macro structure analysis and micro action strategy research, this book focuses on institutional analysis at the meso level. Although the macro structure debate has been and will continue to be controversial, the macro structure analysis appears too static and rigid. Similarly, micro-level analysis of individual organizational action strategies pays too much attention to the strategic mechanism of individual organizational actions, while its theories often appear fragmented. Neither structural debate nor action analysis can explain the pluralistic and dynamic nature of state–society relations in contemporary China.

From the perspective of structure-dynamic unity, this book interprets the pluralism and dynamics of the interaction between the state and society in contemporary China, and transcends the shortcomings of static rigidity and the dynamic fragmentation in the existing research. Under the analytical framework of "Two-way Strategic Interaction between State and Society in Changing External Environment", this book discusses how the continuity and dynamics of the strategic interactions between state and society are possible, and the process of mutual shaping that occurs between the strategic interactions of these two groups and the external environment. In addition, this study focuses on the dynamic discussion of the dual subjects of the government and industry associations and chambers of commerce, rather than the discussion of the single subject of the government or industry associations and chambers of commerce. This approach emphasizes that the relationship between the state and society in contemporary China is not only the result of a single force, but the process of self-adjustment and change in the interactions between the government and industry associations and chambers of commerce.

The findings in this book have important implications for understanding and exploring the future direction of state–society relations in contemporary China. From the perspective of Western scholars, trade associations and chambers of commerce are important political structural arrangements through which entrepreneurs, industrial bourgeoisie, and businessmen can carry out economic associations, obtain various rights, and express their economic interests and thereby form a strong driving force for pluralism and democratization (Moore 2003). Upon examination, China's industry associations and chambers of commerce were no doubt disappointing, because they were more often used as an important tool for the state to absorb the bourgeoisie and "depoliticize" integration. Put another way, the development of China's industry associations and chambers of commerce was meant to better consolidate the existing power of the state (Dickson 2003, 2008; Hildebrandt 2013; Tsai 2007a, b).

Contemporary Chinese industry associations and chambers of commerce, however, can effectively influence policy formulation and implementation, and change government behavior to a certain extent. Examples include Taishun Small Hydropower Industry Association's supervision of Taishun County's Electric Power Bureau administration according to law; Shanghai Indoor Environment Purification Industry Association's prodding of government administrative inaction; Zhejiang Bicycle and Electric Vehicle Industry Association's improvements of government policy responsiveness, etc. At the same time, the government is constantly self-correcting and self-adjusting to better adapt to the needs of industry associations and chambers of commerce and changes in the external environment. This back and forth contributes to the continuity and the dynamics of the interactions between industry associations and chambers of commerce and the government.

The relationship between these groups is one of mutual adjustment through strategic interaction. As Shambaugh said, the country needs equilibrium in adaptation and contraction (Shambaugh 2008, 2016). While the party and the government adjust to changes in the external environment, they are in fact constantly changing themselves, and at the same time industry associations and chambers of commerce have achieved self-growth in their interactions with the government. Therefore, the future relationship between the state and society in China is a pluralistic and dynamic process of opening-up, rather than a static and closed solidified structure.

3 Looking Forward

Future research should explore the following areas. First, the scope of research on the policy participation of industry associations and chambers of commerce needs to be expanded. China is not the monolith of western imagination. There are big differences between local governments and the central government and the country's regions. Research into the policy participation of China's industry associations and chambers of commerce needs to be extended to the national level and should further examine the central and western regions. Second, contemporary China is a rapidly changing and complex research object. This study uses the framework of "strategic interaction between government, industry associations and chambers of commerce in the changing external environment" to explain the pluralism and dynamics of the current relationship between the state and society in China. But this is only a stage or a section of what is the "diachronic nature" of that relationship. In this sense, this study's explanatory exploration of the pluralism and dynamics of state–society relations in contemporary China is only the beginning. Follow-up research on the relationship between the state and society in China needs to make further efforts to expand the research sample and track the temporal and spatial nature of China.

References

Dickson B J. Red Capitalists in China: The Party, Private Entrepreneurs, and Prospects for Political Change. Cambridge: Cambridge University Press, 2003.

Dickson B J. Wealth into Power: The Communist Party's Embrace of China's Private Sector. Cambridge: Cambridge University Press, 2008.

Hildebrandt T. Social Organizations and the Authoritarian State in China. Cambridge: Cambridge University Press, 2013.

Hsu J Y, and Hasmath R. The Chinese Corporatist State: Adaption, Survival and Resistance. New York: Routledge, 2012.

Jing Y. Between control and empowerment: Governmental strategies towards the development of the non-profit sector in China. Asian Studies Review, 2015, 39(4): 589-608.

Kennedy S. The Business of Lobbying in China. Cambridge: Harvard University Press, 2005.

Moore B. Social Origins of Dictatorship and Democracy: Lord and Peasant in the Making of the Modern World. Boston: Beacon Press, 2003.

Shambaugh D L. China's Future. Cambridge: Polity Press, 2016.

Shambaugh D L. China's Communist Party: Atrophy and Adaptation. University of California Press, 2008.

Teets J C. Let many civil societies bloom: The rise of consultative authoritarianism in China. The China Quarterly, 2013, 213: 1-20.

Tsai K S. Capitalism without Democracy: The Private Sector in Contemporary China. Ithaca: Cornell University Press, 2007a.

Tsai L L. Accountability without Democracy: Solidarity Groups and Public Goods Provision in Rural China. Cambridge: Cambridge University Press, 2007b.

Unger J. Associations and the Chinese State: Contested Spaces. New York: ME Sharpe, 2008.

Unger J, Chan A. Corporatism in China: A developmental state in an East Asian context. In Bowles P, McCormick B L and Unger J (Eds). China After

Socialism: In the Footsteps of Eastern Europe or East Asia. Armonk: ME Sharpe, 1996.
White G. Prospects for civil society in China: A case study of Xiaoshan city. The Australian Journal of Chinese Affairs, 1993, 29: 63-87.
White G, Howell J A, and Shang X. In Search of Civil Society: Market Reform and Social Change in Contemporary China. Oxford: Clarendon Press, 1996.
Yep R. The limitations of corporatism for understanding reforming China: An empirical analysis in a rural county. Journal of Contemporary China, 2000, 9(25): 547-566.
Yu J, and Shen Y. Adaptive cooperation: strategic changes in the relationship between the Chinese government and social organizations since the 18th National Congress. Cass Journal of Political Science, 2017, 3: 39-41.

The manufacturer's authorised representative in the EU is Springer Nature Customer Service Centre GmbH, Europaplatz 3, 69115 Heidelberg, Germany. If you have any concerns regarding our products, please contact ProductSafety@springernature.com

Printed and bound by CPI Group (UK) Ltd, Croydon, CR0 4YY
30/09/2026
02225286-0002